why we can't have nice things

Duke University Press   *Durham and London*   2022

why we can't have nice things

Social Media's Influence on
Fashion, Ethics, and Property
Minh-Ha T. Pham

Printed in the United States of America on acid-free paper ∞
Designed by Courtney Leigh Richardson and
Typeset in Untitled Serif and Helvetica Neue
by Westchester Publishing Services

Library of Congress Cataloging-in-Publication Data
Names: Phạm, Minh-Hà T., [date] author.
Title: Why we can't have nice things : social media's influence
on fashion, ethics, and property / Minh-Ha T. Pham.
Description: Durham : Duke University Press, 2022. | Includes
bibliographical references and index.
Identifiers: LCCN 2021053949 (print)
LCCN 2021053950 (ebook)
ISBN 9781478015987 (hardcover)
ISBN 9781478018612 (paperback)
ISBN 9781478023210 (ebook)
Subjects: LCSH: Fashion—Social aspects—Asia. | Social
media—Influence. | Clothing trade—Moral and ethical
aspects—Asia. | BISAC: DESIGN / Fashion & Accessories |
SOCIAL SCIENCE / Popular Culture
Classification: LCC GT525 .P45 2022 (print) | LCC GT525
(ebook) | DDC 391.0095—dc23/eng/20220124
LC record available at https://lccn.loc.gov/2021053949
LC ebook record available at https://lccn.loc.gov/2021053950

Cover art: Opening Ceremony bag, otherwise known as a
"China Bag."

Contents

In the broadest terms, this book can be described as a study of how collective thinking and actions—both coordinated and uncoordinated—produce material effects that don't always bring about the nice things they intend to do.

Collectives of people were also central to the writing of this book but, in this case, their impact on the ideas in it and on me as I wrote it has only been generous and generative. I'm delighted to be able to thank them here.

This book's current shape owes much—and then some—to Tamara Nopper's incisive comments and intellectual insights. Thank you for reading it, getting it, and making it sharper. Huge thanks, also, to Ken Wissoker, Joshua Gutterman Tranen, Ihsan Taylor, and the whole Duke University Press staff, without whom this book would be a pale shadow of itself.

Earlier drafts of this book were guided and transformed by the wonderful conversations and groundbreaking scholarship of the organizers and presenters of the first Race+IP symposium at Boston College in 2017. Thank you, Anjali Vats and Diedre Keller, for welcoming me into this amazing community. I've learned so much from and am constantly inspired by the research and community-focused work that critical race intellectual property (IP) scholars are engaged in, especially the following friends and interlocutors: Boatema Boateng, Rosemary J. Coombe, Carys J. Craig, K. J. Greene, Diedre Keller, Roopali Mukherjee, Madhavi Sunder, and Anjali Vats.

I owe much of my understanding of Indigenous theories of property to the radical thinkers and artists who convened in New York City for the second Race+IP symposium in 2019. It was an honor to imagine and co-organize this meeting with my dear friend Jane Anderson and to learn from Rebecca Tsosie (fellow girl gangster), Chidi Oguamanam, Trevor Reed, and Laura Ortman.

Many thanks to the institutions that invited me to present parts of this project: Brown University, Stanford Center for Law and History, New York University (NYU) School of Law, Bard Graduate Center, University of Washington, and The Factory Contemporary Arts Centre in Ho Chi Minh City.

The Center for Critical Race and Digital Studies at NYU has become one of my most cherished intellectual homes. I'm grateful to be in community and conversation with all of you, especially Isra Ali, Andre Brock, Paula Chakravartty, Aymar Jean Christian, Wendy Chun, Sarah Jackson, Rachel Kuo, S. Heijin Lee, Charlton McIlwain, Lisa Nakamura, Alondra Nelson, Safiya Noble, and Erique Zhang.

My thanks and solidarity to friends and co-conspirators at Pratt Institute, NYU, City University of New York, the New School for Social Research, Columbia University, Cornell University, and beyond who have made New York City an intellectual, social, and political home for me: Jane Anderson, Jon Beller, Jayna Brown, Youmna Chlala, Denise Cruz, Jessie Daniels, Tanisha Ford, Macarena Gómez-Barris, S. Heijin Lee, Amita Manghnani, Christina Moon, Mendi Obadike, Jan Padios, Lauren Redniss, Uzma Rizvi, Noliwe Rooks, Karin Shankar, Ethan Spigland, Brandi T. Summers, Steven Thrasher, and Thuy Linh Tu.

To my family and friends who provided love, care, long walks, and long talks—all of this (and so much more) helped me finish this book and begin a new life chapter, thank you! Tan Pham, Thoda Nguyen, Son Pham, Jina Kim, Hai Pham, Robin Blake, Kathy Azada, Yindy Vatanavan and Chad Beckim, Kelly Chiusano, Đỗ Tường Linh, Melissa Fondakowski, Diarro Foster, Jungwon Kim, Katya and Spencer Lum, Angela Ruggiero, Claudia Scherer and David Limon, Thuy Linh Tu, and Terumi Woods.

Finally, and always, this book is dedicated to Anam. I am endlessly grateful for you.

"Share This with Your Friends":

CROWDSOURCING IP REGULATION

In January 2015, a Vancouver-based knitwear brand called Granted Clothing (hereafter, Granted) found sweaters on Forever 21's website that resembled sweaters of its own design. (The Granted sweater cost between $200 and $350; the Forever 21 sweater cost under $40.) Granted's first reaction wasn't to call its lawyers but to call on its social media followers. In a long message posted on both Instagram and Facebook, Granted accused Forever 21 of a number of offenses, including hiring people "to scour the internet to find original designs without any regard, make a profit and offer no compensation to the original designers" and selling "blatant copies" of sweaters "made here in our Vancouver design studio." The message ended with a plea to social media users "to help us take a stand" and to "share this [social media post] with your friends."[1] (Throughout this book, "social media user" refers to a heterogeneous mix of people using the internet to expose fashion copycats.) The response was immediate and pronounced. The Instagram post received 556 likes and 174 comments. The Facebook post has been shared 179 times and has 71 original comments and many more replies, rebuttals, and counter-rebuttals in the form of actual text and Facebook likes.[2] This is an unusually high level of user engagement for the brand. Its other social media posts sometimes receive no comments at all.

Within twenty-four hours of Granted's call to online action, news about the sweaters gained wider television, radio, and print media coverage and, with it, more social media activity in the form of shares, likes, comments, and tweets from a wider constellation of users, including comic Wyatt Cenac, musician Questlove, and actor Michael Ian Black— celebrities with massive social media followings but who aren't usually associated with fashion. Although a handful of users criticized the brand's hypocrisy—pointing to the striking similarity between Granted's sweaters and the hand-knit Cowichan sweaters that Coast Salish women of Vancouver Island had been creating for generations—the vast majority of users rallied behind Granted by echoing its message or adding to it. For example, although Granted's message doesn't mention the manufacturing origins or conditions of the Forever 21 sweaters, several users assumed—and no one challenged the assumption—that the Forever 21 sweaters were made in "China" or in the "third world" in violation of US and Canadian copyright laws ("it's absolutely copyright infringement, unfair, and I'd think, quite illegal").[3] Granted's statements and hashtags emphasizing the local Canadian production of its sweaters also encouraged this geo-racial thinking in which fashion ethics is a property of the Global North and fashion copycatting is a problem of the Global South.

Facebook users who expressed anything less than full-throated support of the knitwear brand (a tiny minority) were subjected to a range of corrective actions. Those who mentioned the Cowichan sweaters were barraged with counterarguments about cultural appreciation and design inspiration. Those suggesting that copying may not be such a bad thing—that being copied by a retail giant like Forever 21 might provide significant, if unintended, upsides such as increased media attention and brand recognition—were ridiculed as naïve and illogical. Some of the dissenters eventually retracted, qualified, or deleted their statements. Nearly everyone else offered Granted their full support by sharing its social media posts, promising to buy more Granted sweaters, and/or vowing to boycott and vowing to tell others to boycott Forever 21. More than a few users urged Granted to pursue legal action, beginning with, as one user suggested, a crowdfunded campaign: "Start a Kickstarter for lawyer fees. I'm in."[4]

If Granted was concerned that the lookalike sweaters created unfair market competition, then the internet helped it recover its competitive edge. Forever 21 was dragged through the very public mud of a fashion copying scandal; Granted boosted its reputation as a small, scrappy, and ethical company standing up to a notorious retail pirate; and a critical mass of social media users raised the profile of Granted's sweaters (by devaluing the Cowichan sweaters Granted copied and the Forever 21 sweaters that were copied from Granted). Everyday social media practices—liking, tweeting, commenting on a post, and sharing a post—shaped market transactions and outcomes by influencing not only public perceptions but also consumer behavior in Granted's favor.

The Granted case is a prime example of what I refer to throughout this book as crowdsourced intellectual property (IP) regulation. These are the everyday social media activities that emerge around issues of fashion creativity and copying. They take the form of a social media post, a like, a share, a retweet, a comment, or, just as effectively, no comment at all. The lack of "social media outrage" that some forms of fashion copying receive is also doing regulatory work and reveals as much about the rules, norms, and logics of crowdsourced IP regulation as outrage does. Today, social media users are heavily involved in the tasks of indicting, trying, adjudicating, and excusing alleged fashion copycats. Their determinations, while informal and extralegal, have real cultural and material consequences.

As the Granted case illustrates, a broad spectrum of people, including those who may or may not consider themselves "fashion consumers," is being recruited under the subtext, if not the explicit language, of consumer social responsibility to use their social media accounts to police the boundaries of fashion IP and impropriety.[5] Answering and oftentimes anticipating calls like Granted's to "help us take a stand," social media users are naming, shaming, and demanding boycotts against fashion copycats while defending and promoting alleged copycat victims. These kinds of ad hoc, informal, crowdsourced fashion trials by social media— as much as consumption itself—are now understood as ordinary functions of consumers' role in and responsibility to fashion design, the most profitable and valued sector of the global fashion industry.

Crowdsourced IP regulation represents the latest phase of fashion's digital and economic restructuring. It also marks the expanding nature and scale of fashion's unpaid, underpaid, and casualized labor force. In my first book, *Asians Wear Clothes on the Internet*, I examined a more limited use of crowdsourced fashion labor: personal style blogging. Using the global ascendance of Asian superbloggers as an entry point, I analyzed how race, gender, and class shaped fashion work in this informal and casual labor market. I explained how fashion's new system of indirectly and directly sourcing out marketing and promotion services to social media users (e.g., fashion bloggers) overlapped with and departed from the older system of outsourcing manufacturing work to women and girls living in or from the Global South. I was especially concerned with understanding how and why Asians (from very different geo-socioeconomic backgrounds) were disproportionately represented in these externalized labor markets. *Asians Wear Clothes on the Internet* provides an account of the various factors—cultural, economic, and technological—that created the conditions for some Asians to rise to the top of this digital labor market.

Fashion's *latest* digital labor system doesn't enlist only fashion bloggers (a small and self-selected group of social media users); it also encourages anyone with even a passing concern about fashion ethics to provide crowdsourced IP regulation services. This includes fellow designers, online journalists, legal bloggers, and macro-, micro-, and noncelebrities.

The broad base of participation points to several key differences between *outsourced* and *crowdsourced* fashion labor. Whereas outsourced apparel manufacturing is established, secured, and formalized by a legal contract between a brand and a specific factory or factories, crowdsourced IP regulation is underpinned by an informal social market contract. Participants aren't legally bound to do this work; they're bound by ideals and values of ethical fashion. The private nature of outsourced apparel manufacturing—private, in both the sense of "not public" and corporate—renders this work invisible. The terms of the legal contract are not publicly accessible and the work and work conditions are hidden by long, convoluted supply chains and powerful branding. In contrast, the social and public nature of crowdsourced fashion labor is pervasive and hypervisible. In fact, brands benefit from this work only when the work is visible. This is why Granted encouraged consumers to share its social media post with friends. Sharing—or making the post more visible— amplifies Granted's message and sharpens its market-competitive edge at a time when consumers are increasingly basing their purchasing decisions on a brand's ethical credentials. Brands work at and benefit from being seen as ethical. And now social media users are a productive part of these corporate efforts.

But as visible as crowdsourced IP regulation is, it's paradoxically invisible in the sense that it's often illegible as *work*. Online practices of policing the market for fashion knockoffs are so embedded in the everyday practices of social media users that they usually go unnoticed or misidentified. Like fashion blogging, crowdsourced IP regulation is generally seen as a "social media pastime."[6] The mainstream media refers to it as "social media shaming," a practice associated with the internet's broader "call-out" and "cancel" cultures. "Shaming" isn't an inaccurate term but it is inadequate. It implies a reactive stance that doesn't capture the full breadth and impact of the productive work that social media users are doing when they're policing the market for "fake" fashion.

To recognize social media users' regulatory services *as* digital labor—akin to the kinds of work already represented in internet studies—is to highlight how everyday social media activities are being mobilized in the service of fashion capital accumulation.[7] It also allows for a more careful consideration of the various kinds of work social media users are doing when they're "shaming" fashion copycats. Generally speaking, this work involves defining and policing the boundaries between "authentic" and "fake" fashions *that may or may not be illegal*. More specifically, we can divide the work that internet users are doing into three different but interlocking categories.

First, users are doing extralegal work—extralegal, because most social media users who are liking, commenting on, and sharing social media content about fashion copycats aren't IP experts. Their determinations aren't based on legal doctrine and aren't backed by legal enforcement mechanisms. Instead, they're creating and circulating a common sense of legality about fashion design, property, and impropriety that is influencing corporate and consumer behaviors. As I explain later, the extralegal quality of these social media trials is a strength, not a disadvantage, when it comes to regulating the fashion market.

Second, consumers' regulatory actions are doing the work of social reproduction. The crowdsourced regulation of fashion creativity and copying more often than not reproduces and secures Western standards of fashion ethics, taste, and intellectual property. Thus, regulating fashion copycatting—its meanings and practices—is also a means of reinforcing the dominant social, market, and geoeconomic relations that underpin global fashion. Together, the extralegal and social reproductive work that crowdsourced IP regulation does constructs not only a common sense of fashion ethics but also an ideal ethical fashion subject in racialized, gendered, and classed terms. Accused copycats may or may not have violated the law but they're always perceived as having offended mainstream Western, middle-class, and tacitly white sensibilities about fashion ethics. Today, this offense is generally interpreted as a sign of a nonnormative capacity or a racialized incapacity for creativity, for appreciating Western notions of property rights, or for having and exhibiting good taste.

We see the racial aspects of contemporary ethical fashion discourse most clearly in stereotypes about Asians, fashion knockoffs, and their underdeveloped fashion tastes and sense of ethics. Ethical fashion's social contract dictates that consumers share in the responsibility of protecting the purity of the (Western) fashion-design market from the flood of illegitimate/fake Asian products threatening to encroach on and corrupt it.

This leads to the third kind of work that crowdsourced IP regulation does: race work. Popular ideas and attitudes about, say, Asian copycats, Indigenous and ethnic inspiration, and the universality of Western property logics are reproduced and perpetuated anytime social media users call out or defend fashion designers for copying. The callouts and their effects—the uneven distribution of outrage or protection and sales or boycotts they generate—follow racial and colonial patterns. The naming and shaming of fashion copycats do race work by organizing and maintaining relationships to global fashion capitalism along racialized lines. Through crowdsourced IP regulation, social media users have become deeply implicated in global fashion's racialized processes of value creation and value extraction—processes from which they don't benefit as workers or as consumers. That is to say, the idea that there's inherent virtue in choosing to buy the more expensive copy—Granted's copy of the Cowichan sweaters instead of Forever 21's copy—is bad for consumers.

To be clear, recognizing crowdsourced IP regulation *as work* is not the same as celebrating or affirming this work. In fact, the reason to acknowledge it as work is to critique the ways that ethically minded social media practices can serve to perpetuate and legitimize global capitalism's racial and economic inequalities. These inequalities are starkly displayed in the Granted example. Social media users—including the Granted designer—railed against Forever 21's unethical sweaters by racializing them through direct and indirect associations with cheap labor, China, and the "third world." An example of the indirect racialization of Forever 21's sweaters is the designer's repeated emphasis on the superiority of the Granted sweaters' local Canadian production—a tacit way of suggesting the foreignness and inferiority of the Forever 21 sweaters. (In fact, Forever 21 is based in Los Angeles and works with a number of factories in Southern California.)

While internet fashion watchdogs accused Forever 21 of foreign and deviant business practices, they rationalized the similarities between Granted's sweaters and the Cowichan sweaters as admirable (and normative) expressions of multicultural appreciation and inspiration. Cultural inspiration defenses, especially with regard to fashion, often function in neocolonial ways. The Granted example is no exception. In their defense of the Granted sweaters, social media users—again, including the designer—consign Indigenous and ethnic works to the status of a natural resource ("inspiration") or raw material, there for the use and benefit of Western creative output and capitalist accumulation. Consistently, users' assessments of the Granted sweaters' cultural, aesthetic, and ethical value were couched in racial and colonial concepts of creativity, ethics, and property that have been widely accepted as fashion copynorms.

Racial Myths and Copynorms

The popular understanding of what differentiates fashion innovation from imitation has always been underpinned by a set of informal but pervasive copynorms. While professionals in the fashion-design, legal, and media sectors historically have had a heavy hand in constructing and perpetuating these norms, social media has made it possible for nonprofessionals and nonexperts to join these efforts. Today, copynorms serve to cohere highly decentralized and individualized activities of crowdsourced IP regulation. Their function in the broadest terms is to determine which fashion objects and practices to endow with value and which to deny or extract value from.

Fashion copynorms take many forms but there are several dominant ones. An overarching copynorm is the idea that there's an actual, if not easily definable, distinction between fashion knockoffs and fashion originals. The reality though is that fashion copycat disputes rarely involve original designs. (Fashion is, after all, a copy culture.) The direction and outcome of fashion trials by social media often come down to the different meanings and values given to different fashion *copies*, not the difference between an original design and a copy. In other words, internet fashion watchdogs generally are not protecting legally defined original works of authorship. The determinations they make about ethical and unethical fashion design are rarely based on formal statutes about legally protected property but instead on informal cultural rules and standards (or fashion copynorms) that delineate between what are acceptable and unacceptable forms of fashion copying.

That said, we shouldn't draw too sharp a distinction between copynorms and property laws. As scholars like Rosemary J. Coombe and Laikwan Pang have argued, IP law is itself constituted by legal, cultural, and social norms and fictions.[8] One of these is the fiction, as Coombe puts it, that local knowledge is "mere data" and Western intellectual properties are data that have been processed through "the 'information-intensive industries' of a postindustrial economy."[9] (Her use of a computational analogy is nicely apt in this discussion of crowdsourced IP regulation.) Going on, Coombe writes, "Whether represented as nature or as ideas lying in a global commons, the resources and knowledges of non-Western others were regarded as merely the means and material with which Western authors could produce expressive works. . . . Products of nature thus become products of human culture through Western authorship."[10] As it'll become clearer throughout this book, what distinguishes copynorms from IP laws is not their content but who is now doing the work of defining and enforcing the norms. Rather than pay legal experts, fashion brands depend on social media users to do this work—most of whom have no professional training in international or domestic property law and no meaningful understanding of the history and politics of property regimes.

This leads me to a second copynormative idea that needs dispelling or at least clarifying. Fashion trials by social media aren't struggles over formal property rights but instead informal rights to copy or "copy rights" (written as two words). Crowdsourced IP regulation is extralegal work. Social media users—acting as amateur IP and market watchdogs—are determining, enforcing, and distributing informal copy rights, the culturally constructed and socially communicated rights or entitlements to copy based on norms that tacitly prescribe whose designs may be copied (because they're deemed to be traditional or heritage resources that are part of the global commons) and whose designs warrant protection (because they're valued as "property" whether they fit the legal definition of property or not). Although fairness is the intended goal in these ad hoc IP trials, the copynorms that inform them are freighted with cultural assumptions and biases that have the power to shape corporate-fashion and consumer decisions. That is to say, fashion copynorms are social and cultural constructions that have material effects and produce material realities.

We see the evidence of their material force when crowdsourced IP litigation leads to, for example, a fashion brand gaining or losing consumers; a fashion product suddenly flying off or, just as abruptly, being pulled from shelves; or the enhancement, tarnishing, or recuperation of a brand name's or designer's reputation. We can also see it in the production and circulation of racial stereotypes about where innovation and imitation are located and where inspiration can and cannot be mined. The materiality of copynorms is evident in less obvious ways too. Mainstream fashion copynorms are responsible for the lack of outrage and unequal protection given to Indigenous and nonwhite designers who have long been copied by North American and European brands. When fashion copying is defended as cultural inspiration, we see how copynorms and their unequal distribution of informal copy rights follow colonial lines of value creation and value extraction. Finally, the materiality of fashion copynorms can be seen in the coercive force that compels consumers to avoid budget brands for more expensive brands—perhaps more than they can afford—for fear of being seen as and/or internet-shamed for having uneducated or undeveloped ethics, tastes, and desires. It is the same sort of ethical coercion that compels social media users to provide free regulatory services to a trillion-dollar fashion-design industry.

My use of *copynorms* differs from other uses of the term. Mark F. Schultz has defined copynorms as "the social norms regarding the copying, distribution, and use of expressive works."[11] K. J. Greene understands copynorms as a general social attitude toward copyright law and against piracy.[12] For Schultz and Greene, copynorms bear on copyright law in some way—by moderating, reinforcing, extending, or undermining copyright law. (An example of copynorms undermining copyright law is the general social acceptance of downloading music for free.) Positively and negatively, copynorms typically mediate the effectiveness of copyright law. But fashion copynorms, unlike, say, music and literary copynorms, don't stem from or refer to copyright law. They operate in the absence or inadequacy of copyright law.

For all the emphasis the media and public place on the illegality of fashion copies, the legal status of fashion design is far more ambiguous and inconsistent. In many countries, including the United States, Mexico, and Viet Nam, fashion design, in its entirety, is not protected under existing copyright statutes.[13] In other places like Canada, Nigeria, and the United Kingdom, fashion designs may be copyrighted as works of artistic craftsmanship unless they're intended for mass production, in which case they no longer qualify as original works. And, finally, there are countries where all fashion designs are copyrightable as long as they meet certain— and highly variable—originality prerequisites. As Johanna Blakley has explained, the "novelty standard" for fashion copyright is so low in places like France and Italy that a design that differs only slightly from another design may still qualify for copyright whereas the novelty standard is so high in Japan that very few can prove their designs are thoroughly original.[14] In most cases, the law is unusable. But what the law can't do or won't do, social media users are doing very efficiently.

Unlike the glacial pace of the law, the quick-fire communications and rapid proliferation of content on the internet are better equipped to respond to fashion's breakneck cycles. In the time it takes a lawsuit to be filed, to make its way through the discovery and litigation phases, and to reach a courtroom (if it ever does), the particular garment would likely be "out of fashion" and no longer in need of protection. Or as Andrew Goodman, co-owner of Bergdorf Goodman, puts it, "By the time something is copyrighted it's dead."[15] In the same amount of time, social media users can and have compelled designers to issue public apologies for copied garments, pressured retailers to pull stock from their physical and online shelves, and organized the consumer public in impromptu boycotts against alleged fashion copycats.[16] What can take months and years (and tens of thousands of dollars) in legal limbo takes hours and days online—and costs the (accusing) brand virtually nothing. In fact, brands that actively encourage or just benefit from crowdsourced regulation often gain more in cultural and commercial value than those that attempt to resolve these disputes quietly through legal channels.

Crowdsourced IP regulation is so effective that (as we saw in the Granted example) brands are increasingly turning to social media users before— and sometimes instead of—their lawyers to adjudicate design disputes. As Edgardo Osorio, the founder of Italian luxury brand Aquazzura, puts it, "You just have to go public because that's the only way that hopefully somebody will pay attention and something will happen. Because going through lawyers doesn't work."[17] Fashion law professor Susan Scafidi agrees. As she told *Market Watch*, "Designers have little legal protection and instead have to appeal to social norms against copying. . . . In other words, they have to try the case in the court of public opinion and hope that social pressure forces the alleged copyist to do the right thing."[18] Today, it's not uncommon for fashion brands that believe they've been copied to appeal to the public's sense of social consumer responsibility, an implied social market contract that stipulates consumers have both the social media power and *the ethical duty* to protect fashion brands and the global fashion market from copycats. The ethos of consumer social responsibility animates fashion's latest unwaged and informal labor practice even as it obscures its reality *as work*.

As the Granted and Forever 21 example illustrates, it isn't enough that consumers feel bad for Granted. They're being called on in their capacity as internet fashion watchdogs to give their personal time and resources to creating and sharing social media content, mainstream fashion ethical principles, and copynorms. Contemporary fashion ethics discourse links together an ethics of fashion conduct ("be aware of your purchases") with an ethics of social media practice ("share this with your friends"). To be a good fashion consumer is to be a good content producer. As such, strategies for confronting the "fashion knockoff problem" typically involve both market and media-based actions (e.g., boycotting and social media shaming fashion copycats). Internet users serve as a first-line moral, market, and media defense against those who flout fashion copynorms and the racial and capitalist property logics they represent.

This is another reason why "social media shaming" is an inadequate description. It fundamentally misunderstands media's role in online fashion-copycatting disputes. The expression suggests that social media is just a set of tools for protecting the market against fashion copycats. In fact, social media platforms but also many other digital media (e.g., digital cameras, smartphones, 3D printers, etc.) often serve as the means, site, and object of struggle over the meanings and value of legitimate and illegitimate fashion copying.

As many have observed, anxieties related to globalized markets and digital media have paradoxically increased the significance of borders in an era of supposed borderlessness. In the fashion context, these anxieties have found expression in the race-based and class-based stigmatization of fashion knockoffs as material expressions and evidence of an array of border crossings or transgressions. (These include social, market, and media transgressions, the kind hinted at in Granted's accusation that Forever 21's sweaters are products of internet misuse, of "scouring" the internet.) Crowdsourced IP regulation and their social media networks help to reestablish the racialized market relationships, borders, and hierarchies that digital globalization has ostensibly dissolved. As Raymond Williams presciently observed in 1980, "The means of communication are themselves means of production."[19] Social media is not incidental or peripheral to crowdsourced IP regulation; it is the very thing at stake in these online trials. As will become clearer, especially in chapter 2, the contemporary struggles over fashion copynorms are also struggles for control over social media tools, practices, and environments.

Will the Real Copycat Please Stand Up?

In the Granted and Forever 21 example, the rounds of accusations, condemnations, shaming, and sharing that social media users engaged in are typical of the kinds of regulatory work that internet watchdogs are doing for fashion brands. Yet it would be a mistake to understand the case as representative of the many types and incidences of fashion copying that exist. Fashion copying is an ordinary part of the fashion business. It exists in every fashion-market sector from luxury to budget brands. It also has a significant place in fashion education. Fashion students and interns are routinely asked to copy (or "take inspiration" from) others' designs and looks as a part of their professional training. Yet, as the lack of outrage over Granted's unauthorized copies of the Cowichan sweaters exemplifies, only certain kinds of copying are stigmatized and only some disputes go viral. The selectivity of news and social media outrage paints a very narrow picture of what a fashion knockoff is and who is producing it.

Typically, fashion-copying disputes that draw the most news and social media attention involve what can be described as "bottom-up copying," where the alleged copycat has significantly less prestige than the brand being copied (e.g., a "fast fashion" brand like Forever 21 copying a luxury or designer brand like Granted). In instances of bottom-up copying, accusations are issued from above and bristle with moral indignation about the theft of creative property, hard work, and sales. As I detail in chapter 2, today these accusations are also underpinned with racial and specifically techno-Orientalist associations that implicitly or explicitly associate fashion copying with foreign codes of digital ethics and fashion conduct.

"Top-down copying" receives much less attention. In fact, the most common forms of top-down copying often go unrecognized as copying. Popular euphemisms for top-down copying like *creative inspiration*, *homage*, and *cultural appreciation* rebrand what are actually copies into original works of authorship. This was on full display in the Metropolitan Museum's 2015 exhibition *China: Through the Looking Glass*, a show dedicated to highlighting Chinese influence on Western fashion. Almost any one of the featured pieces (fashions by the likes of Alexander McQueen, Givenchy, Valentino, Dior, and Balenciaga) could have been thought to be the work of an Asian designer. Yet those Western designers and collections weren't subject to social media regulation. Words like *copying*, *knockoff*, *piracy*, and *counterfeit* didn't enter into the mainstream news and social media discourse about the exhibition. The social media public that had just six months earlier skewered Forever 21 for copying Granted's sweaters (and which gave Granted a pass to copy the Cowichan sweaters) didn't raise any objections to the luxury-design copies. Instead, professional and lay reviewers generally embraced *Looking Glass* as a reflection of Western sartorial mastery over Asian cultural resources.[20]

This is perhaps the greatest privilege informal copy rights confer: the power to copy without being branded a copycat. Elite Western fashion copycats suffer little to no damage to their reputations or businesses despite the public exposure of their copying. What's more, copying doesn't damage their moral credibility in the fight against fashion piracy.[21] I'm no longer surprised to learn that a vocal antipiracy advocate has single pieces, if not whole collections, "inspired by" East African (frequently, Maasai), Indigenous, and/or Asian aesthetics. The distinctions between (or judgments of) who can copy, whose copies should be protected from being copied, and whose designs are available or appropriate for copying are at the very heart of the system of copynorms that ordinary individuals now play a crucial role in producing and regulating online.

In the exceptional cases where "top-down copying" is publicly acknowledged, the copying is often excused as an isolated lapse in judgment rather than a reflection of a broader cultural or racial pattern of immorality and unoriginality. We saw this happen when Nicolas Ghesquière (at the time, the head designer at Balenciaga) was caught copying a patchwork vest created by the late Chinese American designer Kaisik Wong. An article about the incident published in *New York* magazine actually begins with "Poor Nicolas Ghesquière" and then goes on to describe him as "the beautiful boy wonder" targeted by a naïve and overeager "fashion police" (per the article's title).[22] Others openly defended Ghesquière's right to copy. In one fashion journalist's words, "[Ghesquière's] jacket is actually nicer—so, what's not to like?"[23] There were no articles or blog posts that used the incident to draw broader cultural conclusions about Ghesquière or Balenciaga. For example, no one chalked up the copycat design to the creative shortcomings of French, Spanish, or European cultures. The media and public ultimately shrugged off the incident as nothing more than a designer making use of an "inspiration supply"—a euphemism that manages to both minimize and elevate Ghesquière's copying.[24] (I say more about this incident in chapter 1 in my discussion about the racial and media constructions of fashion property and copy rights.)

Horizontal fashion-copying disputes, say, between two luxury brands or two budget brands, also tend not to attract much public notice at all. They lack the drama of a "David and Goliath" confrontation, and when they're contained to the luxury sector, these disputes may be intentionally kept quiet by those invested in avoiding bad publicity. Highly publicized disputes like Yves Saint Laurent against Ralph Lauren in 1994 and then against Christian Louboutin in 2012 are few and far between.[25] Social media users tend to focus on copying disputes between vertically polarized brands, particularly cases of bottom-up copying. In these instances, the media portrays luxury brands as fighting an ethical battle—rather than engaging in market-competitive conduct—with mass-market brands. The popular "David and Goliath" framework uses morality to assert class and market hierarchies. By associating the (smaller) luxury market with high ethical standards and the (larger) budget market with low ethical standards, luxury and designer brands are constructed as righteous underdogs in a global industry in which they're actually dominant cultural and economic forces.

Selective press coverage and social media outrage have distorted public perceptions not only of fashion ethics and ethical fashion but also of fashion knockoffs—what they are and where they come from. Yet popular perceptions of design legality and criminality (rather than the law) are the primary factors that influence how fashion producers and consumers view, treat, and respond to different kinds of fashion copies. By "legality," I am drawing on Patricia Ewick and Susan S. Silbey's book *The Common Place of Law* and their conceptualization of "legality" as a resource and process that people draw on in their everyday lives. Ewick and Silbey argue that "social interactions within neighborhoods, workplaces, families, schools, community organizations, and the like" are "the common places of the law" and are more influential than legal documents like court decisions, briefs, and legislation.[26] These social spaces produce "a sense of the legal" that shapes people's behaviors, attitudes, and beliefs in relation to the law.[27] In the early twentieth century, powerful fashion companies used the trade and popular press to create the popular sense of fashion legality (the subject of chapter 1). Today, social media users and environments do this work. But how did social media users come to take the role and responsibility of online fashion IP watchdogs? To answer this, we need to review some history.

The History of Crowdsourced Fashion Labor

Fashion's history of crowdsourcing begins around 1999 when ordinary people were invited into the fashion industry through *Sex and the City* (which made Jimmy Choo, Manolo Blahnik, and other luxury labels household names), *Project Runway*, and *The Devil Wears Prada*. These types of shows and films made the rarefied world of high fashion relatable. They also encouraged people who might never shop for luxury fashion to become conversant in its language and culture and to form opinions about the luxury fashion world. At the same time, early blogging platforms like OpenDiary, LiveJournal, and Blogger emerged and gave fashion TV fans the tools and space to express their fashion opinions and assert themselves as amateur fashion experts.

In 2006, fashion bloggers were given, for the very first time, press passes to cover New York Fashion Week. The presence of a tiny and elite group of bloggers was widely viewed by the industry, the media, and bloggers themselves as a magnanimous gesture from an industry that had always held "exclusivity" as a core value. By 2009, superbloggers weren't just being invited to fashion shows: they were courted with premium front-row seats alongside—and sometimes in place of—media and retail heavyweights. (A writer reporting on this phenomenon in 2009 observed in the *Wall Street Journal* that "at the D&G runway show in Milan last week, the chief executives of Saks Fifth Avenue, Neiman Marcus and Bergdorf Goodman were relegated to second-row and third-row seats."[28]) By the end of the 2000s, the telltale signs of the most fashion-forward shows weren't celebrities but instead A-list bloggers, tweet decks, and blogging stations. But those whom the *Financial Times* characterized as the new "cool kids" (with their new cool gadgets) were actually a new class of workers whose largely unwaged internet activities generated enormous value for fashion brands.[29]

For the majority of social media users who weren't granted physical access to Fashion Week, brands provided them with virtual access. In 2010, a long list of designers (including Calvin Klein, Marc Jacobs, Michael Kors, Tommy Hilfiger, and Proenza Schouler) livestreamed their shows to their websites, social media pages, and even, in Alexander Wang's case, a Times Square billboard. Other designers posted minute-by-minute photos and commentary on Facebook and Twitter. Some forewent the live show altogether. Marc Bouwer, Temperley London, and

Reem Acra prerecorded their shows and shared them on YouTube during Fashion Week.

The fashion industry's willingness to provide the public with digital access to exclusive shows and collections can be explained by political and commercial factors related to the aftermath of the September 11 terrorist attacks and a particular ethos of political consumerism that dominated that period. Almost immediately after the attacks on New York City, politicians from George W. Bush to Rudy Giuliani and Willie Brown (the mayors of New York City and San Francisco at the time) portrayed shopping as a civic act of counterterrorism.[30] As Bush put it in a news conference one month after the attacks, "Now, the American people have got to go about their business. We cannot let the terrorists achieve the objective of frightening our nation to the point where we don't conduct business, where people don't shop. That's their intention."[31] Bush didn't specifically mention fashion but the racially gendered implications and narratives of the War on Terror—particularly as they cohered around the figure of the oppressed, burqa-clad Afghan woman in need of specifically gendered forms of saving by the West (whether by military intervention or humanitarian aid)—gave fashion a central place in the popular understanding of everyday counterterrorism. One week later, Giuliani formalized the link between fashion and counterterrorism in a press conference with members of the Council of Fashion Designers of America (CFDA). The press conference launched the public-private partnership called "Shop for America."

These and other similar events reinforced the idea that widespread access to Western fashion was a necessary condition for the possibility of liberal democratic freedoms of self-expression, self-determination, and choice. It was in this moment that celebrity designers introduced a slate of "democratized fashion" that promised to make fashion (the clothes and the industry) accessible to more consumers. One notable effort was Isaac Mizrahi's collaboration with Target—also in 2003. Although Mizrahi didn't invent the "high-low" fashion-line concept, his was the first to achieve general consumer and industry acceptance.[32] This period also saw the rapid expansion of European "fast fashion" brands into US markets. Like the high-low collections, budget fashion trends were widely embraced as material signs and means of democracy. A San Francisco Bay Area resident who was interviewed in a news story about the impending grand opening of the first H&M store in the area characterized it as "'one of the best things about America—we are one of the Western countries of opportunity. . . . I think it's great that someone can say, you know what, I can be great. I can get the elegant car at the cheaper price. I can get the elegant brand name at a good price."[33]

In this period, the "democratization of fashion" was not only a buzzy new media term but also a key cultural value in the popular discourse about fashion ethics. Terms like "cheap chic," "recession chic," and "credit crunch chic" were widely used to describe budget versions of designer fashions sold at stores like Target, Zara, and H&M. These expressions capitalized on wider cultural political sentiments that saw market access and participation as constitutive features of Western democracy—that viewed (fashion) shopping as a democratic right. In this period, those inside and outside the fashion industry believed that market barriers should be overcome, not strengthened. Even the conservative *New York Times* columnist David Brooks promoted "an aggressively democratic sensibility to the world of fashion" where "the distinction between upscale and downscale is exploded."[34] "Cheap chic" was as much a political fashion statement then as sustainable fashion is today. In the early 2000s, "accessible" fashion was both good politics and good business. It provided a new consumer base and renewed cultural relevance for an industry reeling from the cultural and economic impact of the terrorist attacks.

By the end of the 2000s, the mainstreaming of social commerce or the growing use of social media in commercial activities increased the public's access to fashion. But if the phenomenon widely known as fashion's digital democratization gave consumers greater access to fashion brands and designers, it also gave fashion companies greater access to consumers. In particular, social media provided brands access to consumer attention and engagement, highly valued resources of capital accumulation in the internet fashion economy. The livestreams, tweet decks, blogging stations, and front-row seats that gave social media users an insider view of the clothes also cleared a path for them to photograph, write about, share, link to, and otherwise help publicize and endorse fashion brands and fashion collections in and through their social media networks. Fashion's digital democratization created the conditions for fashion's crowdsourcing labor. By inviting consumers to participate in the culture of fashion, digital democratization encouraged consumers to align themselves with the fashion industry, to imagine themselves as a part of the exclusive world of influential fashion editors, designers, models, and tastes.

Rachel Roy's rationale for sharing videos of her 2010 show on Facebook and Twitter offers some insight into the cultural and economic dimensions of the industry's emergent relationship to consumers. Roy says in an interview that the videos were meant to "give people a more 360-degree view of my presentation. It lets people feel like they are on this journey with me and creates excitement and anticipation. . . . Access is important . . . and bloggers help add a level of intimacy and access to my collection."[35] Roy's offer of consumer access offers a chance at upward mobility, a chance to participate in the exclusivity of fashion ("lets people feel like they are on this journey with me"), in exchange for the unpaid labor of fashion blogging. If social media provided new ways of accessing fashion brands, designers, images, and products, then it also created new expectations that consumers participate in the productive activities of the fashion business. In the Roy example, we can see how crucial social media has been as a catalyst for resignifying fashion labor (so that it includes social media engagements with brand messages and messaging channels), for expanding fashion's productive capacities, and for increasing its cultural economic influence on consumers. In short, the development of global fashion has gone hand-in-hand with the rise of social media.

Today, fashion bloggers no longer garner the same headlines or get the same levels of industry attention they used to. One reason is that blogging has been absorbed into the normal business of fashion. Virtually every designer and brand has at least one social media account that enables them to produce and control the kinds of everyday, intimate connections between brands and consumers that fashion bloggers invented. What's more, the work that was once the province of bloggers (which was once the province of journalists, photographers, marketers, advertisers, models, and so on) is now normalized and distributed across a larger population of social media users. Newer and established brands like Betabrand, Everybody World, J. Peterman, and Timberland crowdsource design work from social media users through online design contests and competitions under the pretense of consumer outreach and engagement. As well as design crowdsourcing, brands crowdsource their market research and advertising from consumers by tacitly and explicitly encouraging them to engage in everyday social media activities (e.g., liking, sharing, retweeting, commenting, and reposting). But these kinds of online activities are no longer associated with fashion's digital democratization.

In fact, "democratization" no longer defines the priorities or values of the fashion industry or the fashion public. "Cheap chic fashion" has been displaced by "investment fashion." Whereas budget fashion a few years earlier was celebrated as an ethical fashion good, as a channel for bringing fashion to the people, now it's seen as an ethical fashion disaster contributing to the worst excesses of the industry: environmental devastation, labor exploitation, and, most significantly for this book, fashion copying. Today, economic investments in our closets have become tantamount to cultural political investments in the ethical issues related to fashion production and consumption (an idea captured by the phrase "vote with your dollars"). The conventional wisdom on ethical fashion now dictates spending more, not less, on clothes. (Ironically, designs created from unwaged, crowdsourced consumer labor are more expensive than those that aren't. A plain T-shirt from one of the above crowdsourced brands costs between $40 and $58.)

Mainstream fashion's turn from cheap chic to investment/sustainable fashion wasn't so much an ideological shift as a rhetorical one. The language of democratization, as I've already suggested, obscured but didn't transform fashion's implicit aspirational class politics. In the mid-2000s, the popular rhetoric about fashion's digital democratization offered an aspirational vision to fashion consumers that their unpaid, consistent, and abundant production of fashion-related social media content could lead to, among other rewards, a front-row seat at an exclusive fashion show. The success of a few highly visible Asian superbloggers seemed to evidence the fact that, through this system of crowdsourced labor, anyone could join the ranks of the fashion elite. In the 2010s, with the resurgence of interest in fashion piracy, thanks to campaigns like "You Can't Fake Fashion" (a CFDA and eBay partnership) and "Fakes Are Never in Fashion" (a *Harper's Bazaar* enterprise), fashion's aspirational framework included a moral dimension.[36]

Today, the ideal fashion subject is also a moral authority of fashion ethics. She—still "she"—pays more, not less, for clothes on principle (and, often, on credit). She follows and shares ethical fashion's rule of thumb that a high-priced garment was probably ethically produced in the United States or Europe and that a low-priced garment was probably illegally made in China or "the third world." The conflation of budget fashion with "fake" fashion, and "fake" fashion with an array of legal and moral crimes from creative disrespect and brand diminishment to the theft of labor, sales, and IP to drug wars and terrorism, is so pervasive it appears as commonsense.[37] Formal antifashion piracy campaigns are no longer active but not because the industry's ethical focus has shifted. To the contrary, its concerns have expanded and been distributed to social media users who now constitute a sprawling network of crowdsourced regulators that provide fashion brands fast, free, extralegal, and effective IP support services.

Whether designers recruit social media users to take up their copycat fight or whether users undertake these fights on their own, the work of crowdsourced IP regulation is always irregular, spontaneous, and distributed across everyday internet and social media routines. It is also an unwaged, remote, flexible, and on-demand (or market-responsive) form of digital fashion labor. Social media users engage in voluntary regulatory activities by creating or responding to a social media post, often in between checking emails; while scrolling through Twitter or Instagram; while "liking" Facebook friends' political, personal, and professional updates; and while reading online content as a temporary distraction from their paid jobs.

The casualized arrangements of crowdsourced IP regulation obscure the reality that social media users are doing *work*, activities that produce fashion cultural and economic capital. In fundamental ways, crowdsourced fashion IP regulation evidences the continued encroachment of work and property logics into people's everyday lives. They mark the ever-more-blurred line between enjoyment and exploitation that Tiziana Terranova identified as a characteristic feature of free digital labor—and now this free labor is being done under the rationale of protecting the ethical standards of the global fashion market.[38]

The fashion industry, in particular, has contributed significantly to redefining work beyond traditional forms of waged labor. From unpaid fashion interns to unpaid models or models that are "paid" in cultural capital (prestige) and/or "trade" (e.g., clothes, shoes, handbags) to fashion bloggers who work for likes, much of the work that supports this $1.5 trillion-dollar global industry is unpaid, and many of these workers aren't recognized as part of any labor category, labor history, or labor movement.[39] Crowdsourced IP regulation is the latest phase in the development of fashion labor and global fashion capitalism. Social media users, by investing their time, energy, and attention to defining and regulating legitimate and illegitimate fashion copies, are doing work that shapes market competition, market hierarchies, and market outcomes.

This book results from my long-standing interest in the shifting nature and future directions of fashion work, particularly for what it reveals about how race, gender, and class structure fashion labor markets—and vice versa—under globalization and digital capitalism. Too often, fashion is left out or considered an afterthought in discussions about globalization, digital labor, and the gig economy even while the industry exemplifies these phenomena. As I hope this book makes clear, the global fashion industry and its expanding reliance on social media, crowdsourced labor, and informal labor (both digital and physical) are not only central but critical to these discussions. Crowdsourced fashion IP regulation crystallizes how inequality is continuously reproduced and transformed under different forms of capitalism even as it's obscured by capitalist ideals about creativity, property, and ethics.

This book is also a response to some of the more popular claims, assumptions, and norms regarding how to think about and do ethical fashion. Topmost among these is the idea that crowdsourced IP regulation—a grassroots practice of building popular awareness and support for the IP issues and challenges designers face—makes the global fashion industry more ethical. But in most cases where the public has spoken, the public has gotten it wrong. Because fashion IP discourse is fraught with racist, colonial, and classist assumptions and norms about creativity and copying and property and impropriety, crowdsourced regulation isn't simply "flawed." It can and often does support oppressive structures of power. (This is the focus of the first two chapters of this book.) Without an interrogation of these oppressive legacies, crowdsourced IP regulation can't provide us nice things like *actually* ethical fashion (clothing produced, distributed, and sold under nonabusive, nonracist, and nonsexist trade and labor conditions): it can only reproduce and legitimize these legacies as the common sense on fashion ethics.

The book is organized in two parts. Chapters 1 and 2 highlight the unequal power relations and structures that underpin fashion IP discourses and regulatory norms and practices. Chapters 3 and 4 explore how social media users counteract IP's unequal power structures. Together, these chapters elaborate the overarching thesis of this book that "original fashion" isn't a *thing* but instead a site of struggle over value systems and market competition under the cover of fashion ethics. As we'll see, authentic and fake fashion, creativity and copying are racialized categories, not neutral facts. Historically, fashion brands, international IP governing bodies, and "free trade" arrangements defined and policed the racial boundaries of these categories. Today, social media users have taken up and expanded this work into extralegal areas.

Chapter 1 begins with an analysis of fashion's first large-scale antipiracy effort, a campaign led by the Fashion Originators' Guild of America (FOGA) in the 1930s. Highlighting FOGA's strategic use of the media and consumer guilt, this chapter demonstrates the prehistory of "social media shaming." FOGA's campaign, tactics, and motivations also reveal the corporate roots of mainstream Western fashion ethics. As this chapter explains, contemporary understandings of fashion ethics emerged from US corporate activist efforts to define and enforce intellectual property for the benefit of corporations. FOGA encouraged white bourgeois women to take up its cause by appealing to their class status as guardians of culture and respectability and exploiting their class-based racialized fears about losing this privileged status. Buying FOGA-approved fashions came to be understood and articulated as a civic act of feminist empowerment (reserved for white bourgeois women).

I conclude chapter 1 by considering the contemporary relevance of FOGA's copynorms in both legal and extralegal contexts. Drawing on analyses of more recent disputes involving US and European brands and Indigenous groups in North America, Latin America, and Africa, I demonstrate how fashion IP regulation is a racial project, a means for unevenly distributing rights and rewards—here, the right to copy (with all the benefits and protection that entails)—along racial lines.[40]

Chapter 2 extends the scope of the discussion in chapter 1 to consider how fashion IP regulation is not only a racial project but also a civilizing project. Today's antipiracy efforts are especially focused on the cultural and ethical primitiveness of Asian fashion copycats—a racial stereotype that's sustained in large part in and through social media environments. While this racial formation has new features specific to the digital era (the contemporary Asian fashion copycat is a strange and threatening hybrid of fashion pirate and media pirate), it derives from deeply rooted ideas about, on one hand, Asians' technical superiority and, on the other hand, their cultural and ethical inferiority.

Today, social media users and environments play a pivotal role in producing and spreading this stereotype. To put it another way, the online discourse about ethical fashion is helping to maintain global fashion's racialized hierarchies. The Asian fashion copycat is ethical fashion's quintessential racial other. It's both a target of ethical fashion's civilizing projects and a backdrop against which ethically minded consumers and brands assert the superiority of Western brands and industries—just as Western fashion is losing its cultural economic primacy.

Fashion trials by social media tend to maintain global fashion's status quo but this isn't always the case. Chapters 3 and 4 provide examples of social media users doing crowdsourced IP regulation *otherwise*. In these cases, crowdsourced IP regulation is a practice that challenges dominant notions of creativity and copying, and with it some of the extractive processes of the fashion design industry.

Chapter 3 presents a detailed case study of an unusual social media trial. In 2016, social media users in Thailand succeeded in calling out the Paris-based luxury fashion house Balenciaga for copying the popular Thai "rainbow bag." Using various social media platforms and a practice that I call "hashtag jamming," Thai users co-opted Balenciaga's hashtags— now important branding channels—in an internet meme that exposed the design source of Balenciaga's bag. The meme effectively, if temporarily, reversed the extractive flow of global fashion. As I explain in this chapter, the Thai hashtag action effectively draws payment from Balenciaga (in the forms of attention and information capital) for its unauthorized and uncredited use of the Thai design.

Chapter 4 focuses on the most influential internet fashion watchdog in the world, an Instagram account called Diet Prada, created by Tony Liu and Lindsey Schuyler. (Its Instagram bio simply says "Ppl knocking each other off lol.") Diet Prada is a force in the social media landscape that attracts as much contempt as it does adoration. (At present, it has 2.4 million followers.) But what both its fans and critics miss is the political significance of its critiques about the problem of people "knocking each other off." Diet Prada's refusal of mainstream ethical fashion frameworks, logics, and niceties, I suggest, reflects an alternative—but not perfect—value system for assessing the problem of fashion copycatting.

Almost all matters of fashion ethics are now discussed, negotiated, and carried out online. And, generally, social media activities pursued in the name of ethical fashion are seen as forces for good. But if the work of crowdsourced IP regulation is obscured by its irregular, casual, and voluntary nature, then the harms it reinforces and sustains are often obscured by the internet's neoliberal conceits or what Jodi Dean calls the neoliberal fantasies of communicative capitalism. She defines these fantasies along three lines: abundance ("the inclusion of millions upon millions of voices or points of view into 'the conversation' or 'public sphere'"), participation (the act of "contributing to the media environment"), and wholeness (the idea that the internet is an "open, smooth, virtual world of endless and equal opportunity" for information sharing).[41]

For Dean, the internet's political promise as a tool of participatory democracy is undermined by its capitalist structures—from its corporate owners to its neoliberal valorization of individualism, market-based freedom, and popularity/virality. Online, political messages "become mere contributions to the circulation of images, opinion, and information . . . trying to catch and hold attention, to push or sway opinion, taste, and trends in one direction rather than another."[42] This is the trap of communicative capitalism. "The use value of a message is less important than its exchange value, its contribution to a larger pool, flow, or circulation of content. A contribution need not be understood; it need only be repeated, reproduced, forwarded."[43] It isn't the significance of the message that makes them "stick," Dean writes, it's the volume or virality of the message. "Sufficient volume (whether in terms of the number of contributions or the spectacular nature of a contribution) gives these contributions their dominance or stickiness."[44] This is a perfect distillation of social media's effect on the public understanding of fashion creativity and copying. Copynorms and copynormative assumptions circulate and gain traction online by appealing to a racialized commonsense about the ethical basis of IP protection in general and fashion IP in particular, about public/heritage resources and private property, about Asians and creativity, and about the moral virtue of elite markets. And their repetition and wide circulation—thanks to social media—lend them greater legitimacy. *Nice Things* aims to unsettle the racialized commonsense that structures the mainstream regulation of "ethical fashion" to move toward a critical framework for evaluating not only fashion property and impropriety but also, indeed, the very ethics of fashion and property themselves.

Regulating Fashion IP, Regulating Difference

For about four years, I casually and then deliberately studied the frenzy of social media activity that erupted any time that a prominent fashion brand was accused of copycatting. What's popularly known as "social media shaming" or, more condescendingly, as "the outrage cycle" has become a routine occurrence online and yet, for the most part, these types of events are poorly understood. To begin, these online activities are much more coherent than their names suggest. While atomistic and fragmented, they have histories and politics that give them structural coherence. This chapter highlights the historical context and institutionalization of fashion intellectual property (IP) regulation. I begin with the predigital history of fashion IP regulation in order to draw out the early emergence of fashion copynorms, the operating ideas and values that undergird commonsense knowledge about fashion IP.

Contemporary copynorms took root in the early twentieth century. They were created during an antipiracy campaign organized and directed by the Fashion Originators' Guild of America (FOGA), a trade organization established in 1932. The campaign set out to do extralegally what had not been achieved legally. Between 1914 and 1931 (one year before FOGA was officially established), Congress considered and rejected no fewer than twenty-two proposals to amend Title 17 of the US Code, which would have provided fashion designs with copyright protection.[1] Scholarly research supported Congress's position. Studies in the 1920s and 1930s found that budget copies of upscale designs were actually good for the fashion industry because they prompted the desire for and the creation of new designs.[2] Decades later, Kal Raustiala and Christopher Sprigman developed this point in their theory of "the piracy paradox."[3] The paradox states that fashion's low IP environment has not only *not* hurt the industry, but actually is the reason the industry has thrived. As controversial as some find this theory, the basic idea of the piracy paradox was once the accepted wisdom of the day.

In the early years of the US fashion industry, copying was a standard business practice, and "fashion copyist" was a recognized job category. (Elizabeth Hawes's popular 1938 memoir *Fashion Is Spinach* provides a vivid account of the role that US "fashion copyists" played in building the US industry.) Fashion copies were so widespread and accepted in mainstream US culture that reputable department stores like Bergdorf Goodman, I. Magnin, and Lord & Taylor openly acknowledged the copies on their shop floors. A common promotional strategy was to display fashion copies next to original designs, tacitly challenging consumers to spot differences between the two versions. High-end department stores made and staked their reputation on their ability to acquire premium-quality copies for their elite clientele.

This was the legal, commercial, and intellectual context in which FOGA and its antipiracy campaign emerged. Its stated mission was to protect the "originators of fashions and styles against copying and piracy of styles of any trade or industry."[4] To this end, FOGA deployed a range of direct and indirect extralegal, and sometimes illegal, actions to control the market and insulate its members from market competition. Its regulatory actions involved a set of strong-arm tactics against fashion retailers and manufacturers that it believed were trafficking in cheaper versions of its members' products. These tactics included hiring secret shoppers to spy and report back on retailers' stock; using its connections in the media to publicly name, shame, and stigmatize those companies found in possession of FOGA copies; issuing "red cards" to retailers that violated its rules; and then publicizing its "red card" list as a warning to consumers and manufacturers against doing business with offending retailers or risk being added to the list themselves.

FOGA wasn't actually concerned with or interested in putting an end to *all* fashion copying though. For years, the organization restricted its membership to only elite brands, those that produced dresses "wholesaling at $22.50 and higher" (the equivalent of about $428 wholesale and, conservatively, $642 retail in 2021).[5] Lower-market manufacturers weren't eligible for membership and so weren't afforded the benefits of FOGA's protection. In other words, the rampant copying in the budget fashion sector—*as long as it didn't impact the luxury sector*—was below FOGA's notice.

Copying also persisted in the luxury sector, including among FOGA members—often in direct violation of FOGA bylaws.[6] The organization's first president, Maurice Rentner, was a repeat offender. Arthur Jablow (an apparel manufacturer who later married Rentner's daughter, Bernice) recounts that his father-in-law never stopped copying Paris, even while serving as FOGA president. Rentner made regular trips to France with a copyist whose job was to secretly sketch the Paris collections for Maurice Rentner, Ltd.[7] These trips resulted in volumes of Rentner-labeled products copied from illustrious Paris-based designers like Edward Molyneux and Christian Dior.[8] The contradiction didn't escape FOGA's notice. But according to Jablow, members were not only *not* bothered by the hypocrisy, they delighted in it. "We used to laugh about that, how do you rationalize that kind of thing? All of them were copying from Paris."[9] FOGA's double standard gave elite fashion brands an informal right to copy and reserved that right as a privilege only they could enjoy.

While FOGA members were quietly copying European designs, they were also openly copying non-Western ones. In 1932 at the legendary Waldorf Astoria hotel in New York City, FOGA leaders introduced the new organization, its mission, and their new collections in a well-advertised and well-attended fashion show. The highlight of the show, according to a rave review in *Women's Wear Daily*, was its "major display" of turbans and veils (forms of colonial nostalgia already popular among the most fashionable Parisian women).[10] None of its members, buyers, the fashion press, or consumers considered FOGA's colonial copying of Asian and African designs a contradiction of its stated principles. In fact, the practice was within the tacit boundaries of FOGA's bylaws, which only prohibited members from copying European "imports" and each other's designs.[11]

At its peak, FOGA had 176 members—all women's apparel manufacturers—and cooperative agreements with about 12,000 retailers across the country. The Supreme Court later found that "more than half of [them] signed the agreements only because [they were] constrained by threats that Guild members would not sell to [those] who failed to yield to their demands."[12]

FOGA's tactics afforded it a significant amount of influence in the industry. But fashion copies weren't just an industry norm: they were also cultural norms. It wasn't enough for FOGA to control the supply side of the market; it also needed to influence the demand side. FOGA understood that it would have to shift consumer perceptions and attitudes away from fashion copies. It achieved this by using branding and shaming strategies. FOGA taught consumers to recognize "originality" through the use of a design registry it created and controlled. To register, a "member simply had to submit a sketch and a description of the design along with a signed affidavit of originality."[13] Claims of originality weren't cross-checked or verified. (Anyone wanting to contest a design's originality had to wait until after the garment was produced.) In other words, under FOGA's institutional structure, fashion elites were accorded the presumption of originality. FOGA formalized this idea and privilege materially through a system of authenticity labels.

Garments whose designs were recorded in FOGA's registry were given labels that said "An Original Design Registered by a Member of Fashion Originators' Guild" or "Registered Original With FOGA."[14] The labels functioned as a nonlegal but formal mechanism by which industry elites were able to establish a monopoly on a particular design (a kind of de facto copyright protection) and, more crucially, a monopoly on the power to determine what counts as "originality." For consumers, the labels served as imprimaturs of quality—a nonlegal trademark—that added market and moral value to each garment. Despite the name, FOGA's authenticity labels didn't certify a design's provenance or guarantee anything that could be verified as "original." They functioned as branding tools, marks that added surplus value to already-expensive fashions. By controlling the registry, FOGA controlled the power to define "original design," the public discourse about it, and the distribution of benefits that accrue from being labeled an "originator" (one of these benefits is the presumption of originality).

In addition to giving consumers a market and moral incentive for buying into its definition of "originality," FOGA used various forms of shaming as a disincentive for buying fashion copies. Using the strong influence it had with the fashion press—a power it exercised intermittently with threatened and actual press bans—FOGA launched a media campaign intended to instruct the public on, in Rentner's words, "the devastating evils growing from the pirating of original designs."[15] In a 1936 *New York Times* article, Rentner identified some of these evils when he blamed mass-market manufacturers for the "loss of billions of dollars in available business in the dress industry." This, he argued, "was caused by the standardization of styles and the depreciation of quality in women's garments."[16] Because the fashion industry in New York City was, at the time, "the largest manufacturing industry" in the city, the largest employer of New Yorkers, and the country's primary clothing supplier, the idea that "standardized and depreciated fashions" or budget fashion copies were killing the industry caused national alarm (much like the decline of Detroit's auto industry in the 1970s and 1980s did).[17] FOGA exploited this concern—primarily using guilt and shame—by encouraging Depression-era consumers to align themselves with the upscale fashion sector and assume responsibility for its well-being.

Rentner's loss-of-sales argument was extremely effective and continues to be a dominant narrative in the mainstream thinking about fashion knockoffs. As I explain in chapter 2, the contemporary version of this narrative has new racial and nativist dimensions. The loss-of-sales argument today does race work by producing a discourse about Asians as an unfair, unethical market threat to US and European designs, profits, and global cultural economic power. This is an adaptation of the Asian invasion narrative, now told as a clash between Western ethics and Asian dishonesty. But reports about fashion's demise, in FOGA's time and today, are greatly exaggerated and self-serving. In the United States, the fashion industry has consistently grown since the late nineteenth century.[18] This isn't to say that individual sectors and retailers haven't faced various stages and degrees of expansion and contraction. Instability is intrinsic to market fluctuations and the changes in fashion consumer tastes. Instability is the condition of doing fashion business (a reality that has always affected workers at the lower end of the supply chain far worse than those at the top). But at the time of FOGA's founding and throughout its heyday, the US fashion industry as a whole was growing rapidly.

The US industry's quick and efficient system of producing a broad range of affordable European styles put it in the best possible position to expand during the interwar period, including the Depression years. In fact, it was largely because European fashion houses were struggling with the disruptions and costs of war that allowed the US industry to emerge into global prominence—a point that was not lost on or lamented by US citizens at that time. An article published in *Living Age* magazine included this shockingly provincial perspective on the Nazi occupation of Paris: "The immediate reaction in America has been one of extreme and untempered patriotism. Mayor LaGuardia has without qualification or reservation proclaimed that New York is the fashion capital of the world."[19] Neither the Depression nor World War II slowed the growth of the US industry as a whole. It was during this period (and FOGA's reign) that "the present-day Garment District, i.e. 'Seventh Avenue', was firmly established."[20]

This isn't to say that *all* apparel manufacturers fared well in this period. As with other industries like cosmetics and food, the bargain sectors of the apparel industry outsold their upscale counterparts. This was the real threat to FOGA members: the loss of their profits and market share to manufacturers in the middle- and lower-market tiers as a consequence of economic depression. But the decline of the upscale-fashion sector that FOGA members represented was small relative to the total revenue and output of the industry as a whole. Citing a report on a high-profile lawsuit that Filene's department store brought against FOGA, Sara B. Marcketti and Jean L. Parsons note that, "in the spring of 1936, guild members accounted for only 130 of the 2,130 dress manufacturers in New York and produced only 6% of the total 84,000,000 dresses manufactured in 1935."[21] Moreover, "the wholesale price of 79% of all dresses was $4.75 or less."[22] Recall that FOGA members produced dresses "wholesaling at $22.50 and higher."[23] The false panic FOGA created and its fashion-media networks fomented about the demise of a cherished national industry served as a cover for business elites' actual concerns about the loss of their privileged position in the market. If FOGA's representation of a waning industry was accurate in any way, it was only accurate in the sense that middle- and lower-tier fashion copies threatened the traditional hierarchy between market sectors. Yet it was because of the availability of low-cost fashion (much of which were copies) that the US industry as a whole thrived during the Depression years.

FOGA failed to represent the truth of its policies and practices, but its multimedia campaign nevertheless succeeded in getting consumers to act on its behalf. By buying FOGA and FOGA-approved fashions and buying into its conceptualization of fashion ethics, consumers indirectly regulated the market. What they bought or didn't buy and what they valued or stigmatized served to reinforce not only social and market hierarchies but also the cultural relevance of upscale fashion at a time when the Depression threatened to destabilize all three.

FOGA appealed especially to white women's civic—and civilizing—obligations to act as moral leaders. As a 1932 article in *Women's Wear Daily* about the new trade organization put it, "The women of the country are going to be asked not to confuse low prices, depression, and the like, with an absence of originality. Driving themselves back into the days of 30 years ago is something that has been foisted upon them."[24] This awkwardly worded passage makes sense when we understand that FOGA's articulation of originality encompassed both the quality of a garment and the moral quality of the woman wearing it. "Women of the country," those who embody the race and class ideal of American womanhood, were being asked not to forgo morality in the face of economic depression and in pursuit of low prices. To choose "original" designs wasn't simply to make a market decision but to fulfill a moral and civic responsibility. Choosing the more expensive dress was a "vote with one's dollars" (as the saying goes today) to sustain the gender-normative capitalist development of the country. A negative vote drove the country into economic and social regression. FOGA's fashion ethics offered a model of moral virtue and civic participation that only bourgeois white women could achieve and that working-class women were expected to aspire to.

If FOGA's expensive copies of European designs were constructed as giving affluent white women superior moral and social standing, then budget copies were portrayed as threatening this position. *Vogue* spelled out some of the risks budget copies posed to women in its July 1933 issue: "It is definitely flabbergasting to see your prized original, for which you paid a respectable price, walking down the street in a bastard version on the back of some saucy little blonde who bought it on Forty-Second Street. It is all very well to be told that hers is not really the same dress at all, my dear—think of the inferior materials, think of the bad workmanship. You don't care . . . you are suffering acutely from the disease called 'She's got my dress on.'"[25] The term "respectable price" refers to both respectable women and respectable businesses; their mutual respectability is tied to their shared respect for the moral and market value of elite designs. Within this context, "piracy" involved a double theft. It robbed respectable white women of their individual and privileged social standing ("she's got my dress on") and it robbed respectable businesses of their profits. The *Vogue* article evidences, first, how deeply entrenched class shaming is in ethical fashion discourses and, second, how fashion ethics functioned historically as a means of maintaining existing social hierarchies among women. By identifying bourgeois white women consumers as the primary beneficiaries of "original designs," FOGA gave them a vested interest in promoting its campaign and legitimizing the importance of "original designs."

This marked an early phase of crowdsourcing fashion-market regulation to the consumer public. Middle-class white women in their capacity both as consumer citizens "voting with their dollars" and as writers for influential women's magazines (e.g., *Journal of Home Economics*, *Woman's Home Companion*, *Vogue*, and *Women's Wear Daily*) acted as armchair IP experts. They championed "original designs" as a matter of civic duty and ethical rightness.[26] In doing so, they helped to articulate business constructions of consumer ethics and copynorms as part of a white feminist project of moral uplift. By promoting universal standards and narratives of respectability, bourgeois white women bolstered FOGA's influence in the market as well as their own social standing as moral authorities (who happen to have large media platforms and financial resources generally unavailable to nonwhite, immigrant, poor, and working women).

The previously cited *Women's Wear Daily* and *Vogue* articles illustrate the two poles of FOGA's construction of bourgeois women's relationship to the market. On one hand, it charged them with the gendered and implicitly racial and classed responsibility of securing the nation's cultural and economic future. FOGA and its media allies represented this responsibility as a kind of manifest destiny or burden ("something that has been foisted upon them"). On the other hand, they were seen as vulnerable members and carriers of civilized society, a group that needed protection in a marketplace teeming with implicitly racialized and explicitly classed and sexualized dangers (e.g., "unrespectable" streetwalking women in "bastard" dresses).

In 2010, the paternalistic discourse of fashion ethics expanded inward. Business academics warned and *Scientific American* reported that fashion copies didn't just pose threats to bourgeois women's social standing: they also have "a hidden moral cost."[27] Fashion copies lead women to lie more, cheat more, and engage in other unethical behavior. (Maybe the streetwalking in *Vogue*'s description?) Women were tacitly warned to avoid fashion copies on the grounds that they might "[warp] people's actions and attitudes," ultimately engendering a "counterfeit self."[28] In mainstream ethical fashion discourse, budget fashion or "fast fashion" has come to indicate not only class status but also moral failure.

Such shame-mongering has its roots in corporate activism, specifically FOGA's antipiracy campaign. The trade organization used fear to help manufacture the ethical virtue of its efforts and its members' products. The protective measures, women were told, were ultimately about protecting "respectable women"—that is to say, bourgeois white women—from the racialized "disease" of sartorial and social cheapness. A very similar kind of alarmist rhetoric emerged in post–September 11 antipiracy campaigns. Suzannah Mirghani draws connections between the hypermilitarized language of antipiracy and the pervasive "war on terror" rhetoric to argue that "anti-piracy discourses terrorize[d] the public into needing 'protection.'"[29] In both periods, powerful fashion companies used antipiracy rhetoric to provoke and secure women's emotional and economic investments in expensive brands and, with them, in the capitalist ethos of possessive individualism that links democratic freedom to the values of private property and ownership.

As influential and powerful as FOGA was in shifting the public opinion about fashion copying, its ideas weren't universally accepted as intrinsic truths or even serious principles. Organizations representing the budget fashion sector (where copying was still normative), like the Popular Priced Dress Manufacturers Group and the Dress Creators League of America, were established in part to push back on FOGA's multimedia campaign. In governmental hearings to discuss and establish industry codes of conduct under the New Deal policies of the National Recovery Act, members of these mass-market fashion organizations expressed their increasing frustration with FOGA's market overreach and ethical hypocrisy. Testifying on behalf of mass-market retailers, Melba Dress Company owner Ben Hirsch took a pointed swipe at FOGA's ethical stance against copying. According to public records, he "poked fun" at FOGA members "who like to call their showing original when in fact they are merely representative of the style trend, if not actual copies."[30]

As well as being unpopular among contemporaries, FOGA's methods and objectives were largely out of step and, in some ways, at cross-purposes with grassroots campaigns that preceded and coincided with it. Historically, groups and movements promoting ethical consumption have been distrustful of, if not antagonistic toward, corporate products and interests. From the first campaigns led by nineteenth-century abolitionists who sought to undercut the production of corporate-branded slavery-made products with alternative "free produce" markets to the many examples of internet "culture jamming" in which user-generated "gripe sites" bearing parodied logos and web addresses were used to humorously expose corporate misdeeds, ethical consumer campaigns have tended to harness consumer power for the purposes of advancing social and public policy goals, not corporate objectives.[31]

The 1930s—FOGA's most active decade—were an especially vibrant time in US political consumerism history. Kathy Higgins has described it as "a veritable golden age of countless and diverse consumer activist groups."[32] Yet there's no evidence that FOGA reached out to or otherwise supported other consumer activist efforts of its time, like the "Don't Buy Where You Can't Work" campaign led by Black church and civil rights leaders protesting racist hiring practices, and the Japanese silk boycott led by the League of Women Shoppers (LWS) in response to Japanese military aggressions in China. Unlike FOGA, these campaigns promoted, even if they didn't always achieve, cross-racial and/or cross-class solidarities.[33] The LWS members, who demographically resembled FOGA's market base of bourgeois white women, often used their privileged position to amplify the voices of African American and Puerto Rican women fighting racist hiring and wage practices. The LWS also supported and actively participated in "Don't Buy" protests.[34] FOGA's narrow sense of what constituted an ethically sound market didn't include equal access to the market for racially and economically marginalized people. With unemployment rates that far exceeded white unemployment in the north and south, most Black Americans would not have had access to the luxury bootstraps of FOGA's ethical consumer uniform.[35]

About ten years after FOGA was officially established, the Supreme Court found it guilty of "the direct suppression of competition" and, more specifically, of violations of the Sherman and Clayton Acts (antitrust laws).[36] This 1941 ruling put a stop to FOGA's corporate bullying and marked the beginning of the end of its reign. Still, its influence on the public consciousness endures. It's generally remembered as a hero in the fight for a more ethical fashion industry, and many of its ideas and frameworks remain the cornerstones of antipiracy fashion discourse (e.g., elite fashion's monopoly on the presumption of originality, Rentner's loss-of-sales argument, and the largely unquestioned belief in the moral and market superiority of upscale fashions). More saliently, FOGA's use of media channels and allies to establish normative behaviors around fashion copying have remained the dominant model of fashion antipiracy efforts into the twenty-first century.

In addition to the copynorms that FOGA helped to establish, bad data also play a crucial role in constructing contemporary understandings of fashion IP. According to the most widely cited figures, legitimate brands lose "an estimated $200 billion a year" to unscrupulous copycats.[37] However, this is an *estimated* figure. Sometimes the financial impact of what is generally and imprecisely characterized as the "counterfeit goods industry" is formulated in more vague terms as "$200 to $250 billion" (in the International Anti-counterfeiting Coalition's estimation) or "over $200 billion" (as Representative John Conyers has put it).[38] These sums are derived from another widely circulated (and entirely fake) statistic that counterfeit goods make up "5 to 7 percent"—or sometimes "an average of 6 percent"—of world trade.[39] These figures have been thoroughly debunked yet they continue to be repeated in and by the media.[40]

Studies by the US Government Accountability Office (GAO) also confirm that the reality and impact of counterfeit trade have been massively overstated. In 2007, the GAO estimated that counterfeit goods make up "less than one-tenth of 1 percent" of world trade and that counterfeit clothing and accessories account only for a *declining* percentage of this tiny fraction.[41] The GAO's 2010 report is especially significant because it directly addresses the fake statistic: "The most commonly cited 'rule of thumb' is that counterfeit trade accounts for 5 to 7 percent of world trade, which has been attributed to the International Chamber of Commerce."[42] Referring to a 2008 report by the Organisation for Economic Co-operation and Development, the GAO report concludes that the "metrics underlying the International Chamber of Commerce's estimates are not clear" and notes that, among economists, there's a shared "skepticism over the estimate that counterfeit trade represents 5 to 7 percent of world trade."[43] Similarly, FBI spokesperson Catherine Milhoan admits that "neither the Bureau nor the National Intellectual Property Rights Coordination Center . . . could find any record of how that number [regarding counterfeit trade] was computed."[44]

The US Copyright Office has also weighed in on the larger question of fashion copyright protection. Its statement to the House Subcommittee on Courts, the Internet, and Intellectual Property ends with this unequivocal conclusion: "Proponents of legislation have come forward with some anecdotal evidence of harm that fashion designers have suffered as a result of copying of their designs, but we have not yet seen sufficient evidence to be persuaded that there is a need for legislation."[45] And, indeed, the data from the Consumer Price Index (CPI)—the government's method for measuring price-level changes in consumer goods and services—do not match the anecdotal evidence. In his congressional testimony opposing the fashion copyright bill called the Innovative Design Protection and Piracy Prevention Act, legal scholar Christopher Sprigman presented data collected from the CPI that showed women's fashion markets across a wide range of price points have remained stable and, in one market, even flourished without a fashion copyright law. Describing the period between 1998 and 2011, Sprigman says, "The top decile of dresses increased in price by over 250% over the period. Everything else stood still. . . . [W]e should observe competition from cheap copies depressing the prices paid for the high-end originals. But that doesn't appear to be the case. The high-end branded originals are the only garments that have any price growth during the period—and the price growth of this segment is very healthy indeed."[46] The history of the US fashion industry bears out Sprigman's reading of the CPI data. Despite, and, as many have argued, because of, fashion's low IP environment, US designers continue to design clothes, students continue to fill fashion schools, and the fashion industry—particularly the upscale sectors—continues to grow by staggering numbers.

I'm not interested in asking why bad data and fake statistics continue to circulate—statistics, incidentally, that are based on conceptual models that don't account for the revenue African American, Asian, Latin American, and Indigenous communities lose to largely (but not exclusively) white US and European designers who copy from them without credit or compensation. But others like Suzannah Mirghani and William Patry have taken on this question of fake statistics. Patry's statement in his book on IP-related moral panics is perhaps the most succinct: "The point in the Copyright Wars is not to point to real data—quite the opposite, the data is fake—the point is to create a sense of siege, of urgency, of a clear and present danger that must be eliminated by either Congress or the courts."[47] I mention the misinformation about fashion copying to underscore the point that debates about creativity and copying, appropriation and appreciation, and private property and public resource are not ethical battles but rather cultural and economic power plays. By and large, the legal and extralegal regulations of fashion copies don't make fashion more ethical; they produce, circulate, and reinforce thoroughly racialized codes of behavior, value, and belonging in the guise of ethical impartiality.

As late as the mid-2000s, fashion copynorms were still primarily produced and distributed through media channels shaped, if not controlled by, industry elites: through news articles, press releases, op-eds, and national consumer education campaigns like "You Can't Fake Fashion" and "Fakes Are Never in Fashion" (mentioned in the introduction). Powerful designers mostly based in the United States and to a lesser degree Europe continued to construct and enforce an ethical fashion discourse that represented their interests as being in the universal interest of promoting a fair and free market. Then and now, fashion copynorms function as structural mechanisms. The conditions of market participation and value creation they set function to legitimize and maintain the industry's traditional power structure.

What is new about present-day copynorms is that the work of producing, circulating, and enforcing them has expanded to include individuals outside the fashion industry and fashion media. The shift in production has also altered (in some ways) the politics of this work. Whereas FOGA's media-supported campaign imposed fashion ethics from the top down and the inside out (from industry insiders out to consumers), crowdsourced

IP regulation is multidirectional and often outside-out, from consumer to consumer. Rather than a corporate activist campaign, the extralegal codes of fashion ethics or copynorms are cloaked in the veneer of social responsibility. Consider *Vox*'s description of crowdsourced fashion regulation, or what it calls "internet outrage":

> Social media has become a powerful tool that's helped movements create global waves of change, from Black Lives Matter to #MeToo. Empowering people with what can coalesce into a collective voice also forces giant companies to listen to the masses. A brand can't simply ignore thousands of angry comments if it wants to protect its public image—or its sales. Small designers can't expect copying to stop, nor can they rely on American law to change. They can, however, count on the internet outrage cycle, the speed of which, fittingly, mirrors that of the fast-fashion industry.[48]

The *Vox* article perpetuates popular myths about crowdsourced regulation as a democratic act of consumer politics ("forces giant companies to listen to the masses"), as evincing the need for strong fashion copyright laws, and as a form of extralegal justice that makes the global fashion market more ethical. Also, like most mainstream discussions about fashion copying, it assumes a normative understanding of who is doing the copying ("the fast-fashion industry"), who tends to be the victim of copying ("small designers"), and what "copying" means. Finally, it shares with other popular writings on the subject an overarching, unquestioned, and unarticulated belief in the ethical rightness of the copynorms these social media actions are guided by, reproduce, share, and enforce. What often goes without saying in the popular discourse about fashion copying is the assumption that fashion copynormative principles and standards are universal, politically neutral ethical codes.

The remainder of this chapter focuses on the racial and colonial politics of copynorms and the, frankly, bad politics at work in their online production and transmission. Before getting to that, it's important to acknowledge that the vast majority of social media users engage in crowdsourced regulation in good faith and with good intentions. But they're responding to a glut of misinformation caused in part by the widespread use of fake statistics and legal-sounding but not legally sound terms like "fashion piracy" and the various kinds of "theft" that get attributed to it. Some of the "things" fashion pirates have been accused of stealing include the time, energy, creative incentives, creative property, and potential sales of good, honest, hardworking designers. Copycats are also blamed for depleting the public trust in the marketplace and robbing the industry of its own future. Consequently, "fashion piracy" has come to be understood as a legal problem in need of a legal solution, and consumers are portrayed as "digital vigilantes" holding bad fashion copycats accountable until more enlightened IP laws catch up.[49]

The "digital vigilante" framework constructs crowdsourced IP regulation as individual acts guided by internal ethical convictions. But if we understand intellectual property as a racial project, as critical race IP scholars have long argued, then we have to contend with the fact that these online practices of citizen fashion policing and legitimizing different forms of copying also protect and serve global fashion's existing social, economic, and geopolitical hierarchies. As we'll see, informal IP regulation doesn't make fashion more ethical: it responds in an ad hoc manner to the expanding demands of fashion's racial capitalism.

Race, IP, and the Racial License to Copy

Proponents of fashion copyright often disregard or seem unaware of the racial and colonial history of property. Mapping the links between race, colonial power, and property is at the core of critical race and Indigenous studies of intellectual property rights (IPR).[50] A foundational premise in this field is that whiteness functions as property. In Cheryl Harris's now-canonical essay "Whiteness as Property," she explains that "whiteness is simultaneously an aspect of identity and a property interest, it is something that can both be experienced and deployed as a resource."[51] As such, "whiteness . . . meets the functional criteria of property," a type of possession whose value is constructed through the law and reproduced through social relations.[52] Those who possess the property of whiteness are legally and socially granted the "privileges and benefits accorded to holders of other types of property." These include "the right to use and enjoyment, and the right to exclude others."[53] In other words, property rights constitute a racial project. They function to distribute property rights—and all the social, cultural, and economic benefits that such rights entail—along racial lines.

A crucial but underappreciated benefit, particularly in the context of fashion IP, is the right to copy. The right to copy and, with it, the right to not be branded a copycat and the right to not have your products characterized as knockoffs have roots in a sixteenth-century European legal principle justifying Western imperialism called *terra nullius*, or the Doctrine of Discovery. In the United States, terra nullius was formally established in the 1832 Supreme Court landownership case, *Johnson v. M'Intosh*. Writing the unanimous opinion, Chief Justice John Marshall held that Indigenous people possessed only "a right of occupancy" to land. Without a property relationship to the land, settlers could assume title to any land they discovered because "discovery gave title to the government by whose subjects, or by whose authority, it was made, against all other European governments, which title might be consummated by possession."[54] Connecting the landownership case to IPR, Anjali Vats explains that "the Doctrine of Discovery laid the groundwork for an implicit corollary in the context of IPR. . . . Like the land in which indigenous peoples only hold a right of occupancy, TK [traditional knowledge] is a disordered space that must be tamed and honed by Western science."[55] The colonial legal myth, Vats writes, "creat[ed] a de facto understanding of TK as in the public domain."[56]

In the 1980s, US corporations restructured international IPR legislation. As Martin Fredriksson has shown, pharmaceutical companies like Pfizer and Bristol Myers in particular pushed to expand IPR beyond traditional concerns like an author's economic and moral rights to profit from their work to tie IPR to trade relations.[57] US corporate activism led to the formation of the World Intellectual Property Organization (WIPO, the UN agency responsible for overseeing and developing IPR globally) as well as the inclusion of IPRs in the General Agreement on Tariffs and Trade (GATT) in 1986 and the passing of the World Trade Organization's Agreement on Trade-Related Aspects of Intellectual Property Rights (TRIPS) in 1995. GATT and TRIPS signify, in Fredriksson's words, the "Americanisation of copyright" in the late twentieth century or the internationalization of US definitions and standards of IPR.[58] As such, international IP laws and logics are inextricably linked to the racial and colonial histories of inequality and violence wrought by US systems of property and dispossession.

Although laws no longer explicitly privilege and protect whiteness as property, Western and international IP regimes still operate in ways that give unequal treatment to non-Western and nonwhite cultural producers and objects based on Western legal conceptions like the public domain. The "public domain"—and particularly what Anupam Chander and Madhavi Sunder characterize as our "romance" with the public domain—has allowed for a racial exception to the general prohibition against fashion piracy. The idealization of the public domain as a democratic commons often elides the unequal power relations that underpin cultural production. "For centuries," Chander and Sunder write, "the public domain has been a source for exploiting the labor and bodies of the disempowered—namely, people of color, the poor, women, and people from the global South."[59] The rush to promote and protect the public domain doesn't ensure justice or democracy but instead serves the interests of corporate actors who are better positioned to exploit the rights and resources of the public domain.

In the fashion context, the structural flaws and biases of the public domain are most clearly illustrated in the kinds of fashion copying that go by the names of cultural appropriation and cultural inspiration. These terms tend to be understood as binary opposites but, as we'll see, both forms of copying—so pervasive in fashion that we can call them copynorms—depend on entitlements derived from formal and informal assumptions about the public domain. Such entitlements create the conditions that allow racially marked and Indigenous knowledge, practices, and objects to be copied with impunity, to be treated as if they belong to, in Turtle Mountain Chippewa scholar Jessica Metcalfe's words, a "free bin."[60] The public domain or the free bin confers an informal but valuable license to copy racially marked and Indigenous designs (whether the copying is classified as cultural appropriation or cultural inspiration) that doesn't extend to the copying of white Euro-American designs. The public domain or free bin exemplifies both the racial exception and the racial rule at the heart of IPR discourse and logics. The IPR regime at once protects (white) property and justifies racial extractivism (or the specifically racialized and colonial processes of resource extraction and capital accumulation). That is to say, the racial license to copy isn't antithetical but essential to the structure and operation of antipiracy discourse, including the normative functioning of IP regulation. It isn't just that IP laws, logics, and regulation fail to protect minoritized creators from being copied; they constitute the structural conditions of fashion's racial extractivism.

Let me provide an example.

In 2015, the Tlahuitoltepec people (part of the Mixe group indigenous to Oaxaca, Mexico) accused a French designer, Isabel Marant, of copying blouses they've created and worn for six hundred years—down to the embroidery color and pattern (see figures 1.1 and 1.2).[61] In the media storm that followed, the public (along with the Mixe people) learned that another Paris-based fashion label legally owned the property rights to the Mixe embroidered top.[62] Antik Batik designer Gabriella Cortese applied for and was granted a patent for the design in "late 2013" or "early 2014." It was also around this time that Antik Batik released its collection of similarly embroidered "Barta" blouses and jackets (see figure 1.3).[63]

In the trial, Marant's lawyer countered Antik Batik's infringement charge by asserting an inspiration defense. He argued, in short, that Marant didn't copy Antik Batik; instead, she was "inspired by" Indigenous designs—designs that he characterized as *motifs du domaine public* (public domain motifs).[64] The court found in Marant's favor. What's

FIGURE 1.1. Group of young Indigenous women wearing Mixe embroidered blouses.

FIGURE 1.2. White model wearing Isabel Marant's copycat version of the Mixe blouse.

more, it invalidated Antik Batik's patent, a move that signaled its tacit agreement with the defendant's classification of the Indigenous designs as belonging to the public domain. Many cheered the court's decision to quash Cortese's patent but by designating the Mixe embroidery pattern a public domain design, it doubled down on fashion's racial and colonial extractivist norms. The court legitimized Marant's and Cortese's rights to take the Mixe design and market it under their own brands while also clearing a legal path for future non-Mixe designers to do the same. It also assumed its own right to take the Mixe people's place as the authority for determining the design's status, meaning, and acceptable uses.

In a legal trial intended to determine the rights to an Indigenous design, no member or representative of the Indigenous community was

FIGURE 1.3. White model wearing Antik Batik's copycat version of the Mixe blouse.

involved and no consideration was given to their claim that European copies of their design constituted what Secretary of Indigenous Affairs Adelfo Regino Montes characterized as "an obvious transgression of the Mixe people."[65] In other words, racialized exclusion was a constitutive condition of these legal proceedings. Adding insult to colonial injury, the court effectively reestablished the originality of the Marant and Antik Batik blouses. One of Cortese's claims was that the Marant blouses harmed the Antik Batik label by "creat[ing] a risk of customer confusion."[66] The judge dismissed this complaint by highlighting—in point-by-point detail—the two blouses' individual distinctive features. In effect, the court found both copies to be sufficiently original designs. This is how the law ratifies and protects creativity as a property of whiteness. It restricts the definition of fashion design to include only white cultural practices, even those practices that are clearly imitative. The legal decision legitimized Marant's blouse as a permissible work of creativity, reaffirmed her reputation as a designer, and reasserted her authorial status in relation to these blouses. What the trial sharply illustrates is that creativity is a property of whiteness and, further, that one of the rights accorded to holders of this property is the racial license to copy. Such entitlement is conditioned on the exclusion of racialized others from enjoying the same right and from accessing the material resources and rewards that accrue to it.

In a case involving two European blouses, the court also issued an implicit judgment against the Mixe blouse. Whereas the judge took the time to enumerate the distinctive features of the European blouses, he consistently described the Mixe blouses in general terms as "the traditional clothes of a Mexican village" (*des vêtements traditionnels du village dans la province D'OAXACA, au MEXIQUE*) or "Mexican folk art" (*l'art populaire de cette province mexicaine*). "Traditional clothing," "folk costumes," and "ethnic garb" are racially coded terms that de-skill non-Western designs as cultural and natural rather than artistic and intellectual. In this classification system, non-Western designs are assigned lower symbolic, material, and legal value than European and US fashions, including copy-cat designs.

Antik Batik technically lost the case and Marant was awarded only a fraction of her countersuit for frivolous litigation (3,000 euros, or about US$3,200, as reimbursement for her legal fees). Yet when fashion creativity is a property right in whiteness—a benefit accrued to those who possess the property of whiteness—such properties confer to their bearers a number of rights: the right to use and enjoyment, the right to reputation and status, and the right to expect continued privileges based on whiteness. All of these rights are reproduced and reinforced through the power to exclude "others" from whiteness and subsequently to deny them the presumption and benefits of "creativity," "originality," and "inspiration." Cortese and Marant benefited in material and immaterial ways from the exclusion of Mixe people from the trial, the exclusion of the Mixe blouses from such property categories as "fashion" and "original design," and the exclusive presumption of inspiration accorded to creators who possess the property of whiteness. Under existing fashion copyright law, the Tlahuitoltepec people received nothing for the unauthorized use of their design—no presumption of proprietorship or custodianship, no compensation, and no accountability—nothing except the legally sanctioned prospect of more "inspired" copying.

The Maasai people of northern Tanzania and southern Kenya have experienced a similar pattern of legally sanctioned exclusion and extraction. Their distinctive red checkered textile design, colorful beads, and their name (spelled in a variety of ways) have been copied by more than 10,000 companies from European and US fashion companies, including Louis Vuitton, Diane von Furstenberg, Ralph Lauren, and Calvin Klein, to European car companies like Jaguar. One estimate finds that in the span of a decade "six companies have each made more than $100 million in annual sales . . . using the Maasai name" while the Maasai people have (so far) gotten nothing.[67] Legal and cultural judgments about fashion and property systematically devalue nonwhite creations while making them available to racial capitalist extraction by white creators who are "inspired" to do so.

When the trial ended, Marant fared as well in the court of public opinion as she did in the court of law. Fashion journalists, bloggers, and ordinary social media users immediately backed the court's decision by writing and sharing articles with headlines like "Isabel Marant Wins Case over 'Stolen' Tribal Design" and "Isabel Marant Cleared of Plagiarism Allegations."[68] Typically, fashion trials by media are viewed as stopgap measures, temporary fixes until stronger laws protecting fashion design are passed. But here we see how closely formal and informal regulatory systems resemble and reinforce one another. Indeed, crowdsourced IP regulation isn't outside the ideological apparatus of property law. It illustrates the expansion of property logics and systems into everyday life through media practices and media environments.

The news media and social media—like the French court—entirely forgot about the Mixe people and their original complaint. So too did the designers. According to a source close to the Tlahuitoltepec people, representatives from the Isabel Marant and Antik Batik design firms failed to respond to the Mixe people's multiple requests to meet.[69]

Several months after the *Antik Batik v. I.M. Production* ruling, the Oaxaca Congress conferred protected status on the Mixe design—a gesture that was more symbolic than legal. As Jane E. Anderson explains it, "Mexico a) is not a signatory to UNESCO's 2003 Convention for the Safeguarding of Intangible Cultural Heritage and b) Mexico has not submitted the Mixe's 'intangible heritage' to the Convention Committee for approval to list."[70] The ruling, then, isn't enforceable or recognized in the international IPR community. While a French court's ruling has a bearing on the Mixe people's rights (some in the media even went so far as to interpret the decision as giving the Mixe people permission to produce and sell their own blouses), the Oaxaca Congress's ruling has no reciprocal impact.[71] This exemplifies what critical race and Indigenous scholars of IP refer to as the neocolonial function of international IPR systems.[72]

Given and perhaps owing to the Maasai experience, the Maasai and Kaqchikel Maya people of Guatemala have developed IP policies and procedures that accord with the UN's International Labor Organization's (ILO) Convention on the Rights of Indigenous and Tribal Peoples and its definitions and standards of intellectual property. This provides them with more legitimacy and support in the international community among ILO member-states. But international recognition is predicated on and perpetuates an unequal power relationship. Non-Western people are required to adopt foreign concepts of creativity, innovation, and rights as a condition of respect, recognition, and participation in the global market. China is a clear case in point. The global rise of Chinese cultural industries (from electronics to fashion) is occurring alongside a rise in the country's IP litigation. Laikwan Pang documents that in 2008 the number of IP-related cases in Shanghai rose 43.1 percent from the previous year. "All this," Pang writes, "reveals less about the actual IPR infringement situation in China than the country's willingness to embrace international rules."[73] Such willingness is less a matter of choice than of necessity under the Western-controlled international IPR regime. After all, Western IP logics and values, Pang reminds, "are alienating to China in relation to both its Confucian past and its socialist legacy."[74]

Contrary to popular belief, the international spread of IP rules and procedures hasn't expanded the protection of creative works. It's expanded

Western conceptions of property and power to the detriment of "other ways of knowing, other objectives for knowledge creation, and other modes of knowledge sharing."[75] International IPR governing bodies, policies, and procedures haven't protected minoritized groups, and the exorbitant costs of transnational legal actions often put lawsuits out of reach anyway. Ultimately, it remains up to the conscience of individual Western designers to honor racialized and Indigenous peoples' rights and laws—a bleak prospect if fashion history is any indication. (As I'm completing this chapter, Marant's recent product lines include "Navajo" trousers and a cape "inspired by" the Purepecha community in Mexico.)

Legal and extralegal calls for fashion copyright rarely account for the racial and colonial legacies of US and international IPR systems or the ways that the unequal distribution of property protection—in the informal allocation of rights to copy and to not be copied—already shape the global fashion market. Time and again, we've seen that high-prestige brands and designers don't need IP laws for protection from copycats (or from accusations that they've copied low-prestige designers). In addition, the absence of a legally valid infringement claim hasn't prevented high-prestige brands from effectively incriminating low-prestige brands. Social media regulation and copynorms have provided the same results in less time. We saw this in the introduction's discussion about the Granted Clothing, Forever 21, and Cowichan sweaters. Another example is from 2002 when Nicolas Ghesquière was discovered to have copied Kaisik Wong's 1970s vest design.

After Ghesquière was caught and then confessed to copying Wong's vest, there was the inevitable media storm. But the winds of criticism actually blew in Ghesquière's favor. The media and public's disbelief that a designer of Ghesquière's caliber would copy a little-known Chinese American designer turned into excuses, which turned into defenses championing Ghesquière's professional reputation, creative talents, and finally the superiority of his copy over Wong's original design. As I noted in the introduction, the absence of outrage is also an effective form of crowdsourced IP regulation. Indeed, it's one of the key privileges that come with the racial license to copy.

In 2011, the racial license to copy also protected Proenza Schouler after it debuted its "Navajo-inspired" collection. There were no viral social media campaigns calling for a boycott of the luxury brand and no speculation that the fake Navajo collection hinted at a culturally entrenched white, US habit of copying and stealing. The copycat collection also didn't prevent the brand either from winning industry accolades and awards such as the Council of Fashion Designers of America's Womenswear Designer of the Year in 2011 and 2013 or from generating tens of millions of dollars in revenue. (The company doesn't share its revenue numbers but reports have estimated its annual sales in 2011 to be $50 million—more than doubling its 2010 revenue—and "nearly $85 million in revenue" in 2015.[76])

Like Ghesquière, Proenza Schouler's racial extractivism had the ironic effect of bolstering the designers' authorial status and credibility. A *New York Times* article that appeared on the first page of the fashion section gave the Proenza Schouler design team authorial credit for sparking a Navajo chic trend. Worse, it suggested that the luxury copies provided an important service to Navajo people by saving what is "dwindling" in Navajo culture: "At the sartorial and possibly other levels, as well, the Navajos evoked by Navajo chic may be a dwindling few . . . you won't find many young Navajos in the trappings of Navajo chic."[77]

By invoking the colonial myth of disappearing Indians, it sets the grounds for transferring the authorial reins of Navajo chic to Proenza Schouler. (Disappeared Indians can't be creators.) The article commends the luxury label's derivative collection for preserving a quality of essential Navajoness that Navajos themselves are losing as a result of modernization—represented here in the form of mainstream youth fashion trends. With this casual observation, the *New York Times* recasts Proenza Schouler's racially extractivist project as a practice of white saviorship.

Fashion's racial license to copy is a lose-lose proposition for racialized and Indigenous people. Navajos who wear "lip rings, A&F [Abercrombie & Fitch] logos and Crazy Color streaks" and "favor sensible shoes over flimsy moccasins" forfeit some degree of Navajoness, yet Navajos who wear Navajo styles are excluded from the Western trajectory of modernity.[78] The politics of fashion are rigged. And so are the politics of copynorms when copies of Navajo style are accepted as more representative of (and presumably less "flimsy" than) actual Navajo people's styles.

Social media's regulatory judgments, actions, and inactions are informed by this long history of gendered, racialized, and colonial property relations.

Today, they're also shaped by developments in the contemporary digital and global economies of fashion and labor—namely, Asia's rise in the global fashion economy. China and Korea in particular but also Singapore, Thailand, India, and Viet Nam are becoming important design hubs, luxury markets, and serious competitors in the e-commerce marketplace. As I elaborate in chapter 2, global fashion's racial economic restructuring has had a profound impact on the framing and logics of crowdsourced IP regulation and mainstream fashion ethics.

The Asian Fashion Copycat

Asia's copycat markets—especially China's *shanzhai* industries—have gotten a lot of attention in recent years.[1] Scholars in the United States and Asia in particular have painstakingly examined the social life and political economic context of shanzhai products.[2] They've demonstrated how Asian copies reverse global media and capital flows; challenge Western understandings about the creative agency of underresourced, marginalized people; and trouble Western categories of creativity and copying, innovation and imitation, and the real and the fake. Without romanticizing them, scholars have highlighted the oppositional politics and political limits of shanzhai cultural practices and forms.

A good example of the kind of category trouble that shanzhai products make can be found in Laikwan Pang's analysis of a phony Ferrari in her book *Creativity and Its Discontents*. Interpreting the lookalike car as a countercultural practice akin to Homi Bhabha's notion of colonial mimicry (which "mocks the founding objects of the Western world"), Pang writes, "It becomes very difficult . . . to assign a price to the counterfeit Ferrari. Should it be cheaper or more expensive than a counterfeit BMW? Should it be priced according to its condition and quality (use value), or its brand image (exchange value), or its secondhand market value (surplus value)? It is also more difficult to be certain of the hierarchy of brand names in the world of counterfeiting."[3] Pang goes on to caution that the oppositional power of shanzhai is limited. As an example, she recounts how in 2006 Italian politician Franco Frattini made a dramatic show of blaming China for the fake Ferrari. In fact, the sports car was produced in Thailand, not China. Frattini's mistake reflects the West's long-time association of China with piracy and its tendency to conflate different Asian groups. It also illustrates the limits of shanzhai's cultural power. Shanzhai products may disrupt dominant market and social relations, but they don't subvert them.

Neither the popularity of Asian shanzhai culture nor, for that matter, the broad acceptance of white remix culture (exemplified by figures like DJ Gregg Gillis aka Girl Talk and *Free Culture* author and legal scholar Lawrence Lessig) has done much to change the popular association of Asians with *bad piracy*. As many have pointed out, Lessig's book which promotes "the free culture movement" ("not 'free' as in 'free beer' . . . but 'free' as in 'free speech'") explicitly excludes Asia from its liberal democratic legal purview.[4] Kavita Philip sums up the racial politics of the free culture position this way: "Within the space of three pages, Lessig asserts numerous times, and firmly enough for his followers to understand that Asian piracy is deeply wrong/inexcusable/unjustifiable because of its flouting of bourgeois law and the laws of the free market. . . . Asian pirates thus serve as his limit case: the limit point of difference."[5] The difference between remix culture (good piracy) and knockoff culture (bad piracy) is a racial difference that today is constructed as Asian.

This chapter examines the contemporary racialization of piracy, embodied by the Asian copycat. Of course, I'll focus on the Asian *fashion* copycat but the stereotype isn't unique to the fashion context. For example, it plays a central role in political discourse. Just weeks before announcing her 2016 Republican presidential campaign, Carly Fiorina invoked the stereotype in an interview about education policy: "the Chinese can take a test, but what they can't do is innovate. They are not terribly imaginative. . . . [T]hat is why they are stealing our intellectual property."[6] Fiorina's words perfectly articulate the internal logic of this stereotype. The Asian copycat is a construct rooted in a belief about Asians' cultural and ethical underdevelopment. According to the stereotype, Asians' inability to innovate manifests, at best, as a tendency for rote activities like test-taking (or garment work) and, at worst, an inclination for faking, copying, and stealing "our intellectual property" (IP).

Fiorina received some well-deserved criticism for her racism but the focus on Fiorina obscures how widespread her sentiments are. Political figures both to the left and right of Fiorina such as Elizabeth Warren and Steve Bannon have made similar points in their calls for retaliatory import duties on Chinese and Indian products.[7] Suspicions about Asians' propensity for faking and stealing are also embedded in the intensifying protectionist rhetoric toward China, India, and South Korea. Such threats and actions have been taken in the name of protecting "American" creativity, innovation, and entrepreneurialism—often condensed to "our intellectual property"—from the unfair market and labor competition that Asians are imagined to pose.

The Asian copycat stereotype has a long cultural, political, and labor history. I outline this history below, focusing on the source and durability of this racial figure. My primary concern, though, is its contemporary appearance and function in the social media discourse about fashion IP and fashion ethics more broadly. By analyzing the digital construction of this racial figure (in the digital era and in social media environments), I'm concerned with drawing out, first, the technological and racial character of the stereotype and, second, the ideological work it's doing today. How and why did the Asian fashion copycat become the quintessential racial other to the ethical fashion subject? How are designers, journalists, politicians, and social media users reviving and marshaling an old stereotype about Asians' predilection for mechanical repetition and copying to construct the fashion knockoff problem *as an Asian problem* and, more precisely, as a problem of Asian underdevelopment in the areas of culture, ethics, and fashion taste?

The Asian fashion copycat figure provides a model for understanding the broader ideological work that fashion IP regulation does. It isn't only a racial and white feminist project of differentiation and socioeconomic boundary maintenance (the focus of the previous chapter) but also, as we'll see here, a state, corporate, and popular civilizing project of taste making. The assumption about Asians' underdeveloped tastes for making and buying knockoffs and the concern about how to develop Asians' tastes for Western IP logics and norms constitute a significant part of the contemporary discourse about fashion ethics. To be clear, IP regulation still functions as a racial project but, increasingly, it operates in explicitly developmentalist terms through the figure of the Asian fashion copycat.

News and scholarly articles about the immaturity of Asian ethics and tastes—some of them with headlines like "China's Luxury Consumers Grow Up" (in the *Harvard Business Review*)—exemplify the racially developmentalist framing of this discourse.[8] The central conceit here is that Chinese/Asian people's tastes are in need of maturing and that as they mature or become more refined—that is to say, more oriented toward Western fashion copynorms—Asian people will *grow out of* their primitive taste for fake fashion.[9] Of course, the developmentalist discourse about fake fashion doesn't include an interrogation of the racial assumptions that constitute the category of "fake fashion" or the larger geopolitical economy that structures IP laws and logics. Indeed, the Asian fashion copycat works to rationalize the neocolonial relationship of international labor and trade agreements between Western fashion centers and "developing" or "underdeveloped" Asian fashion peripheries.

Like earlier campaigns against fashion copycatting, the contemporary antipiracy movement is still fueled by white feminist efforts and white feminist beliefs in the free market and IP rights as moral concepts and market participation as a practice of moral agency. Leading figures in the fight for fashion IP include law professor Susan Scafidi, designer Diane von Furstenberg, and legal blogger Julie Zerbo. But fashion IP's developmentalist discourse has also drawn in nonwhite people, including Asian designers, journalists, and state officials who want to prove their "civilized" status and aim to be a civilizing force in Asia.

Angelica Cheung, while acting as editor-in-chief of *Vogue China*, alluded to a civilizing mission in her incredibly condescending characterization of Chinese consumers: "I feel there is a certain sweetness in this lack of knowledge. They were probably working in fields or mines just a few years ago. . . . You don't sneer at these people. You help them and through including them, you educate them better and they will become more sophisticated."[10] Elsewhere, she says, "You need to explain swinging London, Mary Quant, the Beatles and why these people made a difference. If you don't explain, they're just clothes."[11] Likewise, *Harper's Bazaar China* editor-in-chief Sha Xiaoli has said that a primary task of her magazine is to "educate [readers] *from zero* about trends in fashion, culture, art and design."[12] Western products and cultures (e.g., swinging London, Mary Quant, the Beatles) are presented as a means to racial mobility, a way of transcending the crudeness of Asian tastes for, say, conspicuous logos and fake labels to acquire a more sophisticated taste for Western luxury products. Asian fashion magazines are widely represented and viewed as performing a racialized taste pedagogy, as providing (Asian) readers with a (white) "luxury lifestyle education."[13] Of course these magazines also provide their Asian editors and writers something—new cultural roles as well as paid and unpaid jobs as stewards of racial uplift.

Beyond the fashion media, Asian designers and state officials are also taking on these roles in efforts to attract Western foreign direct investments and consumer markets. For example, fashion designer Cai Meiyue told the *New York Times* that Chinese designers need to take ethical lessons from Western designers. "We have to learn from foreign designers— they have a good sense of responsibility and won't copy other designs. It's important to educate our designers and make them aware of the harmful effects of copying others."[14] Later in the article, she attributes this lack of responsibility to Chinese people's underdeveloped sense of fashion taste, a consequence of "centuries of cultural conservativism."[15] Cai's point echoes popular antipiracy discourses and slogans like "You Can't Fake Fashion," an antipiracy campaign launched under Diane von Furstenberg's leadership as president of the Council of Fashion Designers of America (CFDA). In both cases, Western IP principles, norms, and values are universalized through appeals to aspirational fashion desires and goals. To be fashionable—that is to say, to embody Western modernity— is to conform to Western IP norms.

Asian editors, designers, and state officials who make promises about "cracking down" on IP infringement play an important role in ethical fashion's civilizing mission.[16] They perform and promote the local acceptance of Western IP's legitimacy. Louise Michele Newman's book on early white feminism's role in racial and colonial civilizing projects provides a useful analogue here. She describes the "civilization work" that nineteenth-century white feminists did "converting 'savages' to Christianity, 'Americanizing' immigrants in settlement houses, 'uplifting' Negroes for the Freedmen's Bureau, and 'bringing civilization' to Indians on reservations."[17] Nineteenth-century white feminism certainly excluded nonwhite women but it also relied on them and particularly Black women for its legitimacy. Newman writes, "The evolutionist discourse of civilization also had profound significance for women of color, who had

to demonstrate that they too were 'true women' . . . in order to certify that their race already was or could soon become civilized. Black
women reformers offered themselves as models of black womanhood to
prove to white racists that there was nothing inherently inferior about
the black race."[18]

But just as white feminists demanded that nonwhite women measure
themselves by a white, middle-class standard based on the assumption
of their racially gendered inferiority, Western brands demand that Asian,
African, and Indigenous nations conform to Western paradigms of creativity and ownership that necessarily invalidate non-Western notions
of creativity and custodianship. This is the price of entry into the global
marketplace.

Western brands use IP to retain their dominant position in the global
market by wielding Western cultural and legal norms against non-
Western designers, consumers, and governments. This has included
everything from pressuring Chinese courts to uphold Western/foreign
property rights in China to stigmatizing Asian manufacturers and retailers as copycats (while Western brands continue to contract with
Asian garment factories to produce their products).[19] The international,
Western-controlled IP regime continues the neocolonial power relations between fashion centers and peripheries that deregulation policies
began in the 1980s and 1990s. It's telling that fashion peripheries stigmatized as hotbeds of fake goods are commonly described as "the Wild
West" or, in one more overtly Orientalist case, "the wild, wild East" (a
reference to the civilizing discourse of cowboys and Indians).[20] And now
this neocolonial economic order is being reproduced in and through social media.

The people and places of Asia are now so closely—and, as I'll explain
later, automatically—associated with copycatting, knockoffs, and the
class-based assumptions about them (e.g., they're products of cheap ethics, cheap labor, cheap materials, and cheap construction) that a Made in
China label or a Made in Bangladesh/Viet Nam/Korea/and so on label is
enough to cast a pall of illegitimacy over even luxury garments. It's not
uncommon for social media users to make a show of their ethical consumer values by publicly rejecting Asia-made fashions. ("I remember
seeing an Alexander Wang dress for $800 with a Made in China label.
LOL BYE!"[21]) Even the lawyers at the Fashion Law blog wondered about

this with their article title, "Are Your 'Made in China' Luxury Goods Just as Luxurious?"[22] (Their answer is inconclusive.)

And, for some, it isn't just fashions *made* in Asia but also fashions *sold* in Asia that raise alarms. When Martha Stewart tweeted about her trip to China in 2014, users responded with cautionary tweets like "@MarthaStewart I wouldn't trust that you would be getting a bargain. most likely counterfeit goods" and "@MarthaStewart They were all knock-offs to dupe the tourist trade. Don't buy any."[23] Nothing in Stewart's tweets mentioned or suggested she was looking for bargains—much less knockoffs—yet users immediately connected China with fashion knockoffs. The copynormative equation of Asia with knockoffs also operates in the reverse. As we saw in the social media discussions about the Granted / Forever 21 dispute (in the introduction), garments judged to be "knockoffs" are assumed to be made in China or, as some users put it, manufactured in "the third world." This, despite evidence that Forever 21 produces a significant portion of its clothes in Southern California factories and despite the reality that long, dense, and convoluted supply chains make it impossible for consumers, and oftentimes brands themselves, to verify a brand's manufacturer, much less the manufacturing location of particular garments.[24] What's more, the location tells nothing about the conditions of production or who made the clothes. A garment "made in Italy" may well have been made by Chinese workers in any one of the Chinese factories in Prato, Italy, where, in 2018, three-quarters of the city's approximately 4,400 garment factories were Chinese-owned and -operated.[25]

The reason that fashion copycatting is associated with Asians is not because anyone believes that all Asian people or only Asian people copy but because of the way Asianness has historically signified in Western cultural imaginaries for centuries. As early as the seventeenth century, Spanish missionary Domingo Navarette remarked, "The Chinese are very ingenious at imitation. They have imitated to perfection whatsoever they have seen brought out of Europe. . . . [T]hey have counterfeited several things so exactly that they sell them inland [as] goods brought out from Europe."[26] At the core of the Asian copycat stereotype, then, is a racial trope about Asian mechanicalness, a racial tendency toward rote repetition and nonmeaningful or unthoughtful production. There's no shortage of examples of Asian mechanicalness or techno-Orientalist constructions of Asian difference. Some of the most popular ones were created in the last century.

Perhaps the most well-known techno-Oriental copycat is Fu Manchu, a character created by British novelist Sax Rohmer in 1913. Fu Manchu is an evil scientist who, as Elaine H. Kim observes, is "a figure of towering intellect [who] has mastered Western knowledge and science without comprehending 'Western Ethics.'"[27] Since Rohmer's time, representations of Asians as technically advanced and culturally, socially, and ethically backward have only proliferated. Accounts of Asians appropriating—that is to say, pirating—"Western knowledge and science" but not assimilating to (white) Western cultural norms and social values circulate widely in cultural and political arenas. They also underlie concerns about Asians "taking over" tech industries and universities (especially science and engineering departments). Stereotypes ranging from the Asian coolie to the model minority to the IP thief are all variations on the same theme of Asian mechanicalness or the idea that Asians aren't fully human.

As these examples suggest, Asian mechanicalness is freighted with racial ambivalence and racial suspicion. Although the stereotype has given Asians a relative advantage in certain labor markets—low-wage and labor-intensive jobs in agriculture, electronics-manufacturing, and apparel-manufacturing sectors as well as task-oriented, low-management jobs in corporate sectors—it has also given rise to histories of anti-Asian policies and practices. Techno-Orientalism helped usher in the period now known as the Asian exclusion era, defined by a succession of anti-Asian immigration laws targeting Chinese and then later other East, West, and South Asians.

A vocal proponent of Chinese exclusion was California senator John F. Miller. In 1881, he proposed a law barring Chinese workers from immigrating to the United States by characterizing them as "machine-like . . . of obtuse nerve, but little affected by heat or cold, wiry, sinewy, with muscles of iron; they are automatic engines of flesh and blood; they are patient, stolid, unemotional . . . [and] herd together like beasts."[28] In 1911, sociologist Edward Ross added to Miller's Chinese superworker theory by advancing another theory about Chinese "superbabies."[29] For Miller, Ross, and their contemporaries, Chinese people were not just foreign but alien. Miller characterized them as "inhabitants of another planet"—a popular sentiment that echoes the then-common ethnic slur for Chinese people, celestials. Miller's proposal eventually passed, and the Chinese Exclusion Act was ratified in 1882, the second time the United States denied immigration to a specific group of people. The first was the Page Act of 1875, which targeted Chinese women immigrants.

In the 1900s, racial anxieties about "machinelike" Chinese existed alongside and overlapped with anxieties about mechanical Japanese people. Jack London's 1910 essay, "Yellow Peril," differentiates whites and Japanese people in human and robotic terms. In his words, whites possess "a sympathy and comradeship and warm human feel, which is ours, indubitably ours"—such humanness "cannot [be taught] to the Oriental as we would teach logarithms or the trajectory of projectiles."[30] A Japanese person, according to London, is a "marvellous imitator truly, but imitating us only in things material. Things spiritual cannot be imitated; they must be felt and lived . . . and here the Japanese fails."[31] The stereotype of the technically capable but soulless Japanese person was undoubtedly a reaction to Japan's growing imperial power but Japanese people in the United States were also subjected throughout the twentieth century to the repercussions of nativist social and legal violence.

The success and efficiency of Japanese American farms, fisheries, and other agribusinesses were especially viewed as threats to white labor, white land entitlements, and white safety (due to rumors that Japanese American farmers were secretly spying for Japan).[32] From the 1910s to the 1940s, a series of laws were enacted to thwart Japanese economic and labor efficiency. These included the various US alien land laws, which prohibited "aliens ineligible for citizenship" from owning or leasing agricultural land, and, infamously, Executive Order 9066, which dispossessed approximately 120,000 Japanese people in the United States of their property, their homes, and their civil rights and imprisoned them in remote camps across the country.

By the late 1960s, Japanese mechanicalness signified a threat not just to white land entitlements but also to entitlements to white intellectual properties. Japan's global reputation as a techno-pirate nation was solidified when a company then known as Totsuko and now called Sony introduced "the world's first home VTR—a monochrome reel-to-reel machine" that allowed users to "record [television] programs while they were out."[33] Sony followed up its VTR with the U-matic and in 1975 with the Betamax, or what Universal City Studios characterized as a piracy machine.[34] By the 1980s, Hollywood and Japan were embroiled in a "video war" that would culminate in a Supreme Court trial known as the "Betamax case," or *Sony Corp. of America v. Universal City Studios, Inc.* (1984). Predictably, the publicity around the Betamax case was sensationalized with racist and nativist language that conjured images of invading pirates and yellow peril. A public letter signed by the actor Charlton Heston and sent to key congressional allies warned that a "'group of wealthy, powerful Japanese electronics firms' had 'invaded' the country. . . . They were 'trampling' laws and 'threatening one of America's most unique and creative industries.'"[35] Around the same time, *Foreign Affairs* published an article that singled out Japan as the only nation to become a major economic power by being "imitators" and not innovators. (Only European and North American countries were identified as "innovator" countries.[36]) Between the video and auto trade wars, the Asian IP pirate in the 1980s had a distinctly Japanese identity. As Keith Aoki writes, "Japanese—and increasingly Asian—businesses were regarded as ruthless, unethical, insidious, and unfair competitors, stealing patents and trade secrets, pirating US intellectual properties, dumping products on foreign markets, and engaging in 'un-American' or 'foreign' (in a distinctly pejorative sense) monopolistic practices."[37]

In the 1980s, Japanese people weren't just associated with an unnatural technical prowess: they were, in David Morley and Kevin Robins's words, "virtually synonymous with technologies of the future—screens, networks, robotics, artificial intelligence, simulation." The authors continued: "As the dynamism of technological innovation has moved eastwards, so have these new technologies become subsumed into the discourse of racism. As these technologies have become associated with Japanese identity and ethnicity, they have reinforced the image of a culture that is cold, impersonal and machine-like. The barbarians have now become robots."[38] *Gung Ho*, Ron Howard's 1986 film, represents and resolves this widespread racial economic anxiety through a comic narrative about a culture clash between rigid Japanese corporate managers and a ragtag team of Pennsylvania autoworkers. While *Gung Ho* concludes with a reassuring civilizing message that Japanese workers can actually learn to be more human, what it and other techno-Oriental narratives share is a racial developmentalist suspicion about Asian mechanicalness.

It's worth remembering that while the US media from the late 1960s through 1980s represented Japanese businesses as IP predators and thieves, it also praised Japanese and Chinese Americans as "model minorities" whose purported success in the United States was used to refute claims of anti-Black, anti-Chicano, and anti-Latino racisms.[39] Representations of Asian pirates and model minorities don't contradict one another. They're different sides of the same Orientalist coin in which Asian superhuman/alien/foreign capacities to work efficiently, repetitively, and tirelessly are both the subjects of Western fear and fantasy. Economic efficiency, as Colleen Lye has put it, is "the most salient feature" of Asian stereotypes.[40] If an Asian propensity for unrelenting work has been admired in and by the West—this, combined with gendered stereotypes about Asian feminine docility helped make Asia the garment factory of the world—it has also been vilified as an unfair competitive economic and/or labor threat.

At the turn of the twenty-first century, Western perceptions about Asian mechanicalness had found a new focus in Asia's seemingly unstoppable growth in consumer and e-commerce markets. Almost daily, media outlets in Asia, the United States, and Europe published stories about the rapid expansion of Asian online retailers into broader regional and global markets. The most popular e-tailers include Alibaba (China) and its consumer-to-consumer portal Taobao, Rakuten (Japan), YesStyle (Hong Kong), RomWe (China), Pomelo (Thailand), and Stylenanda (Korea). All have developed a broad and diverse consumer base by establishing corporate headquarters in Asia and the United States and/or by developing strong online marketing programs (e.g., internet banner ads, Facebook ads, and keyword-search ads). The most powerful among them, Alibaba, competes successfully with the likes of Amazon and eBay and is worth more than Facebook, Amazon, and IBM *combined*.[41]

In 2019, the Asia-Pacific region led global e-commerce growth.[42] As of this writing, China is leading Asia in e-commerce sales, followed by Japan, Taiwan, South Korea, and India (in that order).[43] With US malls and big brand retailers like Sears, Macy's, and JCPenney shuttering or filing for bankruptcy in record numbers (nearly 7,000 stores closed in 2017 alone, a 200 percent increase from 2016) and, on the higher end of the market, closings for Barneys New York, J. Crew, and Neiman Marcus (in 2020), many believe that we're in the final days of Western economic hegemony and US retail dominance.[44] A joint report from the management consulting firm McKinsey and Company and the media outlet *Business of Fashion* declared 2018 "an important tipping point" year when "the West will no longer be the global stronghold for fashion sales."[45] The findings of this report are consistent with the existing research on global retail, which shows that Asian markets are far outpacing US and European markets. Fashion sales in China, Hong Kong, India, Indonesia, Malaysia, the Philippines, Singapore, South Korea, Taiwan, Thailand, and Viet Nam combined have grown more than 600 percent between 2001 and 2016.[46] Together, these economies generated $6.6 trillion in sales in 2016 or almost double the value of US sales ($3.9 trillion).[47] China and Viet Nam lead the pack in terms of growth rates (although Viet Nam's impact globally is still small).

There's no consensus on the long-term effects and scope of what some are calling "the Asian Century" (and even that name is a bone of contention).[48] But what is *not* a matter of debate is that Asian fashion brands and consumer markets are becoming major players in the global fashion market as a result of years of governmental and private investments focused on building Asia's digital and cellular infrastructures and expanding the public's access to smartphones, mobile internet, and social networking and social commerce apps. Although Asia's economic growth has slowed since 2018, new government initiatives to strengthen online marketing, merchandising, and payment systems in rural China and Southeast Asia, particularly Malaysia, Thailand, and Viet Nam, mean more not less Asian e-tailers and markets are on the horizon. Southeast Asia's e-commerce economy more than doubled between 2015 and 2018 and is expected to "hit $240 billion by 2025, which is $40 billion more than previous estimates."[49]

Asia's ascendancy in the global fashion economy is directly tied to digital media and its ability to lower barriers to market entry. It is also an unintended side effect of long-standing international trade and IP agreements that made Asia the world's factory for about half a century. After decades of providing the labor power for Western fashion capitalism, Asia has acquired a technically experienced workforce and a technically complex infrastructure, which allows it to now compete against the very firms it has been making products for.

Indeed, it's no coincidence that the most popular Chinese copycat products originated in Shenzhen. Shenzhen was one of the first Special Economic Zones to be established in China in 1978 when Deng Xiaoping launched the Reform and Opening Up policy. Shanzhai commodities are an unintended but entirely predictable consequence of globalization. Think of them as global capitalism's chickens coming home to roost. As Fan Yang writes about shanzhaiji or copycat mobile phones, "Not only did the large factories set up in [the Shenzhen] vicinity benefit from state policies favoring foreign direct investment (FDI), they also brought a large number of (predominantly female) peasant migrants from inland Chinese provinces to Shenzhen in search of jobs in the export processing sector."[50] Not surprisingly, workers hired to produce Western branded products often parlayed their skills and knowledge to moonlight in the shanzhai factories.[51]

This was the point that Alibaba cofounder Jack Ma was trying to make when he famously, if indelicately, said, "Fake products today are of better quality and better price than the real names. They are exactly the [same] factories, exactly the same raw materials but they do not use the names."[52] Ma's words both play into and shatter the stereotype of the Asian copycat by rearticulating the racial value of Asian products (as superior in quality and price). Not that everyone appreciated his point. Gucci American, Inc., and Michael Kors, for example, have openly protested Alibaba; Kors called it "our most dangerous and damaging adversary."[53] Well before Ma provoked the ire of Western fashion, though, many already viewed Asian e-commerce companies as sites of Asian copycatting and sources of knockoff "scams."[54] After all it was the Western fashion design and media industries that invented the contemporary version of the Asian fashion copycat.

When Fashion Piracy Meets Media Piracy

There's a certain irony in the timing and nature of today's antipiracy sentiment. At a time when digital technologies have made copy (-and-paste) cats of us all and when content sharing is widely recognized as a legitimate use—if not *the* defining feature—of digital media, fashion copycats are being singled out as external to mainstream copy culture. *Asian* fashion copycats are a special source of concern.

In particular, Asians' "misuse" of digital technologies is seen as the crux of the fashion knockoff problem. Countless examples of this technoracial narrative are scattered across news and social media sites. One of the more prominent examples includes a *New York Times* front-page exposé on fashion knockoffs, which focused exclusively on an Indian American businesswoman named Seema Anand. Anand's New York City–based company Simonia Fashions supplies clothes to a wide range of retailers from Forever 21 to Bloomingdale's. The choice to spotlight a virtually unknown Asian designer is significant. By omitting more famous and successful knockoff manufacturers like Allen Schwartz (owner of the US company ABS) and Nick Beighton (CEO of the UK-based ASOS, or "As Seen on Screen"), the article constructs the fashion knockoff problem as an Asian problem with all the Orientalist tropes of secretiveness, unscrupulousness, greediness, and foreignness that typically constitute cultural representations of "the problem Asian" (the underside of "the good Asian" or model-minority stereotype).[55]

The Asian knockoff artist is one of the most visible "problem Asians" today. Since around the mid-1990s, sensationalist news stories about federal and local policing agencies raiding informal retail spaces like the mobile vendors on Canal Street (which partially runs through Manhattan's Chinatown in New York City) have primed the public to associate fashion piracy with Asians and their illicit social and economic networks. But the *New York Times* article goes beyond the usual racial construction of the knockoff problem. The big scoop here is the techno-Orientalist story it supposedly reveals. Anand isn't just another Asian knockoff artist: she's an Asian knockoff artist armed with technology and no scruples about how to use it.

The article begins by describing Anand as a mysterious figure who's had a disproportionately large impact on the luxury fashion market: "Ms. Anand . . . is a designer few would recognize, even though she has dressed more people than most of the famous designers."[56] She's also represented as an outsider: "Ms. Anand . . . will be following the catwalk shows through photographs posted instantly on the Web" (rather than in person, by invitation). The suggestion that Anand has gained unwarranted access to luxury fashion through digital tools and digital content is repeated several times, conflating media piracy and fashion piracy. As we'll see, contemporary fashion piracy discourses often equate stealing designs with stealing digital content. The article charts the fashion knockoff problem as a straight line from Anand's web browser to her email to the factory computers in India, which are equipped, we're told, with "programs that approximate the design of a garment from a Web image without the need to pull apart the seams."[57] If Asian labor was considered mechanical before the internet (void of emotion, expressivity, and creativity), it is now imagined as fully mechanized in the digital age ("without the need to pull apart the seams"). This technoracial tale has become the master narrative in contemporary discussions about the fashion knockoff problem, now so pervasive that it often goes unquestioned.

Designer Lazaro Hernandez gives a similar account of the fashion knockoff problem in his 2011 testimony supporting the Innovative Design Protection and Piracy Prevention Act (ID3PA). (This was the same year that Hernandez's label Proenza Schouler introduced its Navajo-inspired collection.) Reading from a prepared statement, Hernandez describes the knockoff problem in this way: "Digital photographs from a runway show in New York or a red carpet in Hollywood can be uploaded to the Internet within minutes, the 360 degrees images viewed at a factory in China, and copies offered for sale online within days—months before the designer is able to deliver the original garments to stores."[58] Hernandez appeared before the Judiciary Committee of the US House as a representative of the most powerful fashion-trade organization in the United States, the CFDA. The CFDA has been lobbying for a fashion copyright bill for decades and played a significant role in crafting and increasing support for the ID3PA. (In 2007, CFDA president Diane von Furstenberg authored a *Los Angeles Times* op-ed urging Congress to enact the Design Piracy Prohibition Act, a forerunner to the ID3PA.[59]) It's a fair bet that Hernandez's statement was CFDA-approved, if not CFDA-coauthored. Either way, I read his testimony as an institutional expression of the technoracial logic underpinning mainstream fashion IP discourse.

Hernandez isn't the first designer to reference "360 degrees." It's a cliché of modern retail. The term suggests that digital technologies have expanded the capacity of companies and consumers to see things that they couldn't see before. Consumer databases and inventory-tracking systems, for example, give companies a real-time view of dynamic and elusive consumer-spending habits, tastes, and sales patterns. Digital videos and video-sharing sites give fashion consumers clear views of once-exclusive runway shows. "Three hundred and sixty degrees" usually implies access and transparency. Recall from the introduction that Rachel Roy's decision to post videos of her runway shows on social media (the year before Hernandez's testimony) was driven by her desire to "give people a more 360-degree view of [her] presentation" and to provide them a sense of "excitement," "anticipation," and "access." Hernandez's reference to the 360-degree view echoes Roy's statement but implies something entirely different—a potential for vulnerability not an offer of openness. Roy's imagined viewer is a racially unmarked (so tacitly white) woman and a trusted digital media user. Hernandez's imagined viewer is Asian and technically untrustworthy. For Hernandez, digital media isn't a means for providing interested fans insider access to a designer's creative process but the means by which mechanized Asians are trespassing into a world for which they're not ethically fit.

Technoracial concerns about Asian copycats reveal the racial and class politics at work in the construction and regulation of "ethical" fashion design. Billions of Asians operating machines (within and outside Asia) have been a significant part of the US fashion industry since around the 1980s. Yet their labor—racially gendered as mechanically docile—has generally not raised any ethical questions for the fashion establishment until now. This reveals two insights about Asians' acceptable relationship to global fashion: first, this vast Asian and predominantly female labor force is *in* but not *of* the industry and, second, their being in and not of the industry is conditioned on their willingness to support without impeding Western fashion's goals of market expansion and capitalist accumulation. The developmentalist logic of fashion ethics limits the Asian Global South to the role of being mere instruments and not agents of creative production.

Scafidi echoes Hernandez's statement almost verbatim in Elizabeth Cline's highly acclaimed book, *Overdressed: The Shockingly High Cost of Cheap Fashion*: "'Today, people can look at the pictures online from a fashion show, which are posted almost instantaneously, and copy them directly in a factory in Asia,' says Scafidi. 'And the photographs are so good. You have photographs in three hundred and sixty degrees. You have photographs in high-definition on which you can zoom in and see what kind of buttons they used.'"[60] Scafidi's statement, unlike Hernandez's, carries the weight of a legal opinion. But that's where the differences end. Both statements reproduce the dominant technoracial narrative that links fashion knockoffs to Asian people and places through digital technologies as well as through vague insinuations of techno-Oriental primitiveness and digital malpractice.

The contemporary Asian copycat stereotype presents a new variation on the digital divide discourse. While the former digital divide is understood as resulting from poor and nonwhite people's lack of access to information and communication technologies (ICTs), the new digital divide is perceived as a consequence of poor and nonwhite people's overly easy access to ICTs and their misuse, abuse, and corruption of these technologies as a result of their primitive IP ethics and values. More specifically, the new digital divide discourse draws a sharp distinction between Western innovators who are seen as using ICTs productively and non-Western imitators who aren't (or whose uses of ICTs get in the way of Western productive processes). Despite their major and minor differences, what the new and old digital divide discourses share is their reliance on long-standing developmentalist narratives of (white) technical progress and (nonwhite) technical backwardness.

In the digital era, the Asian copycat stereotype is produced through not only digital cultural constructions of racial mechanicalness but also digital processes of racial difference. In October 2018, I performed two searches using the key phrase "copycat culture" and a Google Boolean search for "copycat culture AND." (I chose "copycat culture" because of its buzzword status in the public discourse about fashion copying.) The searches were performed on my laptop and another laptop I had never used before. In each set of searches, identical dropdown lists of autocomplete suggestions popped up midway through typing. And in each list, all but one of the suggestions mention an Asian country or business (figure 2.1). Eight months later in June 2019, I re-ran the same searches on a brand-new, unused laptop. This time, a slightly different set of suggestions appeared. What remained the same was the Asian bias (figure 2.2).[61]

Curious about how a more guided query might get around the algorithmic Orientalism, I searched for variations of Italian/Italy copycat culture, French/France copycat culture, and US/American copycat culture—with and without quotation marks. Not surprisingly but somewhat stunningly, in each case Google either redirected my search back

FIGURE 2.1.
Screenshot of two
Google searches
for "copycat cul-
ture" and "copycat
culture AND,"
October 2018.

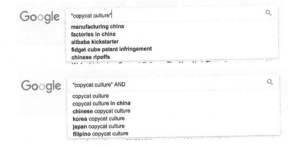

FIGURE 2.2.
Screenshot of two
Google searches
for "copycat cul-
ture" and "copycat
culture AND,"
June 2019.

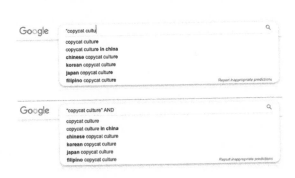

to China—with suggestions for Chinese-related key phrases—and/or offered a list of articles in which the top results focused on Chinese copy-cats (figures 2.3 and 2.4). The tacit message to someone searching for information about copycat cultures is that China is the most reasonable place to begin looking.

Broadly speaking, autocomplete suggestions are generated through a complex and proprietary set of encoded procedures that account for dynamic factors such as the overall popularity of a search, individual search histories, language, and location. Autosuggestions can also be determined by the *unpopularity* of a search. Google has had to modify particular lists in response to user complaints about the racist nature of some of its results. Of course, complaints aren't the only reason Google updates its algorithms. Google's predictive text algorithms are constantly being revised in response to new individual and collective user information. These variables result in the differences between autosuggestion lists on different computers and across different times and places. (The same is true for search-result lists and other automated query systems.) What's

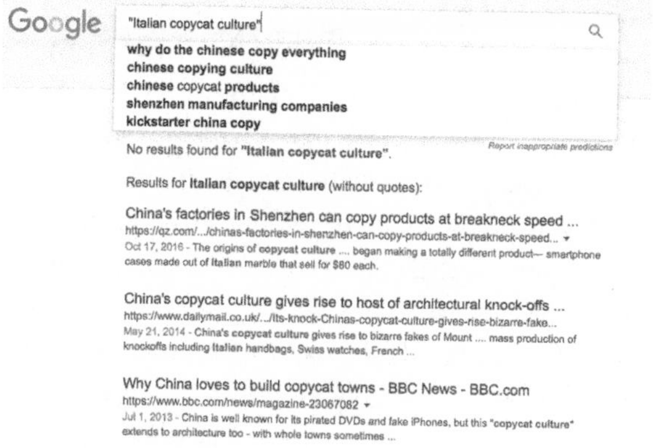

FIGURE 2.3.
Screenshot of
Google search
results for "italian
copycat culture,"
June 2019.

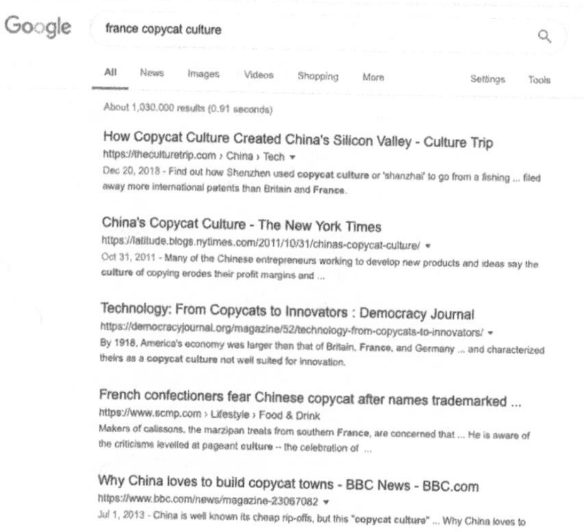

FIGURE 2.4.
Screenshot of
Google search
results for "france
copycat culture,"
June 2019.

significant about these lists, then, isn't any one particular suggestion item or data point but the racial pattern that emerges across multiple data points or the racial information these patterns communicate.

As we've already seen, internet search engines didn't invent stereotypes about Asian copycats and copycat culture. However, when racial stereotypes are produced and shared online, they take on different meanings and functions. The contemporary Asian copycat stereotype isn't generally viewed as a racial developmentalist stereotype but instead as a culturally aware (if not culturally sensitive) explanation of moral difference. Consider the *New York Times* article "Why Do the Chinese Copy So

Much." Like this headline and article, the premise of the Asian copycat is routinely accepted without question or qualification. The stereotype's depoliticization is especially acute in algorithmic suggestions. Seemingly generated without human intervention, automated recommendations of all kinds appear to be immediate (or unmediated), objective machine calculations of the most relevant, most popular, and most useful information. Autocomplete suggestions portray the Asian copycat stereotype as an aggregate of commonsense ideas and beliefs. This is how algorithms shape public discourse about fashion copying. In Tarleton Gillespie's words, algorithms help to "establish and confirm standards of viable debate, legitimacy, and decorum."[62] Through algorithmic processes, a racial stereotype is recoded as data, as objective information.

The contemporary construction of the Asian copycat—as the product of cultural and computational codes—reflects what Peter A. Chow-White has termed "the informationalization of race" or a new paradigm for race that "emerges in discourses of the information age that present themselves as color-blind."[63] The Asian fashion copycat stereotype functions as a coded discourse of race in which racialization operates through the apparently race-neutral language of digital ethics, IP competency, sophisticated tastes, and cultural attitudes toward property and impropriety.

The Asian copycat formation, I suggest, "mark[s] another stage" in what legal scholar Cheryl Harris calls "the evolution of the property interest in whiteness."[64] It simultaneously masks and maintains the persistence of whiteness as property in which the presumption, privilege, and benefits of cultural inspiration are valuable assets that white designers have come to expect and rely on and that nonwhite designers are excluded from. This is not to say that designers of color are not inspired by other cultural forms and ideas but that they're rarely afforded the *presumption* of cultural inspiration, a presumption of trust that confers a host of material and immaterial assets such as the racial benefit of the doubt and all the reputational, cultural, and financial capital that may come as a result of those benefits. Asian fashion makers, in particular, work under the presumption of imitation, not inspiration.

The naturalization of Asian copycatting stereotypes is so pervasive that they have become both common and uncontroversial. On social media, "made in Asia" now has a general pejorative use for designating not only things but also people as being fake (e.g., "Shes [sic] so fake I bet if you look in the back of her neck it says made in China").[65] Award-winning authors like Paul Midler also perpetuate copynormative stereotypes that associate Asians with fakeness or copycatting. Midler, a longtime resident of China, and a seemingly full-time explainer of what's wrong with China, flatly states that copycatting is embedded in Chinese culture: "China's counterfeit culture runs deep."[66] (His most recent book, actually titled *What's Wrong with China*, includes a chapter that characterizes China as a nation of liars.) The fashion-trade journal *Women's Wear Daily* (*WWD*) describes a *"culturally ingrained* piracy problem in China."[67] We find the same racialization of copycatting echoed and amplified in international newspapers where articles with headlines like "Copycat China Still a Problem for Brands & China's Future" (*Forbes*); "Why South Korea Is the Home of Counterfeit Culture" (*Business of Fashion*); "Why Do the Chinese Copy So Much"; and "China's Copycat Culture" (both in the *New York Times*) are no longer surprising.

Such stories, now so popular they might constitute their own genre, typically trade in racial stereotypes and vague accusations. For example, the *Business of Fashion* article about South Korea's counterfeit culture doesn't offer any examples of IP infringement. In fact, the article contradicts the headline. The Korean products it mentions bear generic rather than trademarked names ("the label of the jacket reads 'Classic Fashion' instead of 'Saint Laurent'"). Legally, then, there's no danger of consumer confusion and no harm to the goodwill or distinctiveness of the brand (the reason for trademark protection)—not that this is a concern for Korean consumers. In the words of Alec Leach, the fashion editor of an influential German-based streetwear blog, "It seems that a lot of Koreans aren't really aware of what they are wearing."[68] Another way of putting this is that Korean consumers aren't focused on the labels, making counterfeiting unnecessary and the headline misleading.

By the time a social media user discovers this—assuming they read the article before commenting on it and sharing it—the stereotype about ethically deviant Asians implied in the headlines will have already generated value for the website through a page view, a shared link, and/or increased visibility among the user's social media networks (all sources of ad revenue). This is a key difference between copynorms produced and circulated in social media and those produced and circulating in nondigital contexts. Social media–generated fashion copynorms are productive—specifically, they're racially productive information that creates several kinds of value. First, as I already mentioned, copynorms are racially productive information in the sense that this racial information generates more social media interactions (a necessary condition for advertising revenue on social media). For example, the production and circulation of such information drive social media engagement on Reddit and Quora (two popular question-and-answer social media platforms) where a significant number of discussion forums begin with topic questions like "Do you agree that Korea has a copy culture?"; "Why and how does China rip off everything?"; and "Why do the Chinese copy literally everything?" (I haven't found any comparable forums on why white people copy so much.) The subject or problem of the Asian copycat also generates a significant amount of digital information and social media engagement through eBay discussion forums, Facebook, Instagram, Twitter, personal and community blogs, and online news sites.

Second, racialized fashion copynorms have produced new consumer values. Today, being an ethical consumer means holding and sharing racial stereotypes about Asian retailers and products made in Asia. One of the most frequent questions I see consumers asking on a brand's social media page or the customer feedback section of an online retail site is whether a product is made in Asia. This has become a kind of shibboleth of ethical fashion consumption that's performed, broadcast, and adopted throughout social media and e-commerce sites. Increasingly, brands are preempting this question by publicizing their "local" production directly on their website or by qualifying the Asian production of their products as being exceptionally ethical. (In fashion discourse, "local" is a nonracial but no less nativist code for "not Asian.")

Finally, racialized copynorms produce value for fashion brands that embrace and can embody dominant definitions of fashion creation and authorship. The information that social media users produce when they share thoughts, criticisms, and links about knockoffs—whether cheap Chinese and Vietnamese knockoffs or more expensive Korean "supercopies"—is now a productive source of value accumulation for Western fashion companies. This is why fashion brands tacitly and directly encourage social media users to do this work. At its most effective, crowdsourced IP regulation can increase a brand's market-competitive power by diminishing a competitor's name, reputation, consumer base, and inventory—often by associating the budget brand's products with Asian manufacturing. Zara (Spain), Urban Outfitters (United States), Topman (England), and Lindex (Sweden) are just some of the retailers that have removed copied products from their inventory in response to public pressure.[69] At its least effective, crowdsourced IP regulation reinforces and normalizes the racial commonsense of fashion ethics.

Today, even people who have little interest in fashion will be familiar with the basic tenets and racial expressions of dominant copynorms. The most prominent are that fashion knockoffs are made in Asia, are produced cheaply, and are products of cheap ethics. These aren't separate value judgments. They're intertwined along a chain of race- and class-based associations that cohere around the image of an underdeveloped Third World Asia as the archetypal site of cheapness (e.g., cheap labor, cheap ethics, cheap quality products, and a cheap regard for all of the above).

Knockoffs, it should be clear by now, don't represent "things." They're struggles over cultural economic power that are obscured by fashion copynorms and the practices and rhetoric of ethical washing. The Asian copycat, the embodiment of several copynorms, glosses over the structural realities that condition Asian "knockoffs"—namely, the unequal transfer of resources, wealth, and power that international trade, labor, and IP policies enable. The stereotype diverts attention away from these structural realities and toward racial and developmentalist ideas about Asians' ethical and cultural inferiority.

In the popular and professional discourse about fashion copying, the label Made in China/Bangladesh/Viet Nam/and so forth isn't just a geographic indicator. It is an indication of any number of dodgy (if not illegal) practices with regard to the garment's design, production, and sourcing. This is how social media influences fashion-market dynamics and outcomes. The production and spread of racialized information about ethical and unethical design, real and fake fashion, creativity and copying pull global fashion's center of gravity, which is shifting toward Asia back to the United States and Europe, by appealing to a racialized code of ethics or fashion copynorms.

If there are still any illusions about social media as a radically democratic space, the widespread production and circulation of the stereotype of the Asian fashion copycat should dispel them. Social media may enable more connectivity between and among companies and consumers (including between Western and Asian brands and consumers) but it's also closing off the meaning, value, and practices of cultural production and consumption. The online production and regulation of fashion ethics territorialize the internet as a space of Western capitalist cultural production while making new racial subjects and new racial threats out of those whose practices are excluded from the normative conceptions of the Western capitalist IP regime.

That said, social media engagements and architectures are also enabling new ways of challenging the racial developmentalist assumptions of Western IP regimes and mainstream fashion ethics. These are the subjects I turn to next.

How Thai Social Media Users Made Balenciaga
Pay for Copying the Sampeng Bag

In March 2016, the biggest news story about Paris Fashion Week didn't come from any established fashion-media outlet like *Women's Wear Daily* or any of the *Vogue* magazines published in Paris, New York, London, or Milan. Instead, the hottest news story about one of the most anticipated fashion events of the year originated on the personal Instagram and Facebook pages of social media users in Thailand, who used the social networking sites to broadcast their own reviews of the Balenciaga Fall 2016 ready-to-wear collection.

In the days leading up to Paris Fashion Week, there was already a lot of media buzz about the Balenciaga show and its new creative director, Demna Gvasalia. Fashion insiders wondered how Gvasalia, a designer known for exorbitantly high-priced streetwear (e.g., $1,200 hoodie sweatshirts and $1,100 denim miniskirts), would carry on Balenciaga's tradition of architecturally inspired eveningwear. Once the show was over, seasoned fashion journalists mulled over Gvasalia's mash-up collection. Pieces like ski and motorcycle jackets cut and draped as opera coats received a lot of attention. Younger journalists considered some of the more exciting technical features of the show, including the use (and eventual malfunctioning) of 3D-livestreaming technology.

But social media users watching from Thailand zeroed in on the rainbow-striped tote bags on Balenciaga's runway. What Western viewers didn't know and Balenciaga didn't mention is that the luxury bag was a near-exact replica of the oversized plastic carryalls seen all over Thailand. The multicolored striped bags made of plastic and nylon—sometimes called *sampeng* bags after the Bangkok market of the same name—are more colloquially known as "rainbow bags." Their size and durability make them popular choices as laundry bags, shopping bags, and makeshift luggage. In Thailand, a single bag costs as little as 75 baht, or the equivalent of $2.10 in the United States; Balenciaga's version costs over $2,500.

Gvasalia is not the first luxury designer to get caught copying or even the first to copy an Asian carryall bag. In 2007, as creative director for Louis Vuitton, Marc Jacobs copied the so-called Chinatown shopping bag. Louis Vuitton's copycat version, just like the original, was a large, square-shaped carryall in a distinctive plaid pattern print. The main difference between the two was the very conspicuous Louis Vuitton stamp embossed on the side of the copied bags, a blatant act of taking ownership. Six years later in 2013, designers Phoebe Philo (for Céline) and Stella McCartney (for Stella McCartney) copied Marc Jacobs by also using the distinctive plaid print. On both the Céline and Stella McCartney runways, white models were dressed—sometimes from head to toe—in the print that came to be (wrongly) known as Chinatown plaid.[1] Media and public reactions to the European copies ping-ponged between celebrating them as cultural inspiration or disparaging them as cultural appropriation.

In the previous chapters, we saw how the presumption of cultural inspiration (with its reliance on a colonial construction of the public domain) is a privilege of whiteness that confers to and reserves for its beneficiaries an array of material and symbolic resources. In the Balenciaga example, we can see how its binary other—the presumption of cultural appropriation—is the same white privilege. Both the presumptions of cultural inspiration and appropriation, like whiteness, are constituted by what they are *not*—not piracy, not faking, not knocking off, and not evidence of group-based cultural and moral deficiencies. While there was plenty of disagreement about whether the Louis Vuitton, Céline, and Stella McCartney tote bags were products of cultural appropriation or inspiration, no one described these European copies in racially loaded terms like "knockoffs" or "fakes." In other words, both sides of the cultural appropriation/inspiration binary provides its beneficiaries with exclusive rights to use, enjoy, and culturally and financially profit from others' designs without incurring the racialized costs of being branded a copycat.

If Gvasalia was not the first designer to copy an Asian tote bag, the Balenciaga copy certainly garnered the most media attention, thanks to Thai social media users' informal regulatory actions. Once the Balenciaga show ended, Thai users wasted no time identifying and broadcasting the Thai source of the Balenciaga bag. On their social media accounts, they posted photos of themselves—fashionably smiling and fashionably unsmiling—with the original Thai rainbow bags. The settings varied but tended to emphasize informal everyday scenes: people wearing the bags or otherwise posing with them on the street, in a mall, in a public transit terminal, standing against a nondescript wall, or, in classic blogger fashion, in an overgrown grassy field.[2] All of the social media posts—what I'll collectively refer to as the Thai/Balenciaga meme—were labeled with at least one but usually many descriptive and/or interpretative hashtags written in English and/or in Thai. At least one of the English-language hashtags included the Balenciaga name (e.g., #Balenciaga, #BalenciagaThailand, #Balenciagabag). Through the production and circulation of the meme, Thai social media users linked the Thai rainbow bag to the Balenciaga name.

The meme provides a useful case study of crowdsourced intellectual property (IP) regulation from below. I use *below* because the meme originated in the Global South, in a country located in the periphery of the global fashion economy at the "bottom" of the apparel supply chain. Also, it was created by fashion consumers (and internet users) with low market power to speak truth to a fashion powerhouse that is invested in and profits from a deeply embedded racial capitalist system that extracts marginalized people's knowledge, labor, and cultural heritage resources for its exclusive benefit. And while social media communications about fashion and fashion discourse more generally tend to be in the global language of English, the Thai/Balenciaga meme was mostly produced and circulated in a "local" language (with the notable exception of the word "Balenciaga"). As we'll see, Thai social media users' responses to Balenciaga's copying are shaped by the reality of their marginalized position in the fashion center/periphery hierarchy. Crowdsourced regulation from below doesn't guarantee a radical politics, much less a racially and economically just outcome—and that's certainly the case here. But it does illustrate that the power of the corporate-driven international IP regime and its associated copynorms is not universal, absolute, or secure.

This chapter focuses on how Thai internet users used the Balenciaga hashtag and what the impact of their hashtag actions were. The media coverage of the meme in the United States, Europe, and Asia mostly ignored or glossed over its data aspects. Instead, mainstream media outlets focused on the meme's visual elements: social media users' poses and the presence and location of the rainbow bags. By missing the significance of the hashtags, the media also missed the point of the meme. Overwhelmingly, they interpreted the meme as a celebration of inspiration—as Thai social media users celebrating their culture's sudden status as the source of fashion inspiration. For example, the headline of a *Cosmopolitan* article about the meme asserted that Thai social media users were LOVING (in all capital letters) the Balenciaga bag and that the meme emerged from Thai people's desire to generate "their very own Balenciaga vibes using the 'Sampeng bags.'"[3] Similarly, an *Elle* magazine article declared, "Balenciaga's Striped Bags Are Already #Winning Instagram."[4] Not surprisingly, the US and European media repeatedly described the Balenciaga tote bag in terms of inspiration, as "Thai market stall–inspired" bags; as bags that "appear to be inspired by . . . shopping bags popularly used and sold . . . in Thailand"; and as bags that "take inspiration from cheap totes."[5] Much of the Asian coverage included some of the same interpretations, describing the meme as an expression of pride in having a piece of Thai culture featured on the global stage of a Paris Fashion Week show and in being elevated into a luxury object.[6] However, a few Asian media outlets also noted the meme's critical edge, interpreting the meme as an expression of ridicule and mockery, not admiration. In the words of a Malaysian journalist, Thai social media users were "hav[ing] a laugh at Balenciaga's expense."[7]

Both celebratory and critical interpretations overrely on visual analyses of the meme. And by focusing on the images of Thai social media users and the tote bags, the public discourse emphasized the intentions of the Thai mememakers. What were they doing with those bags? Were they celebrating or mocking Gvasalia/Balenciaga? But online memes are not only visual but also data forms of cultural production. Mememakers aren't just making images; they're also creating data. To be sure, all acts of crowdsourced IP regulation—like all social media campaigns—are coordinated efforts of data production but the Thai/Balenciaga meme's heavy reliance on hashtags invites a specific focus on the data work that crowdsourced IP regulation depends on and, more particularly, the data work that the meme does to recalibrate fashion's symbolic and material economies.

In this discussion, I'm less interested in ascribing a single or coherent intention to the mememakers. Thai social media users certainly don't share a uniform opinion about Balenciaga or an opinion that can be taken as representative of a singular "Thai" perspective about the rainbow bag, the Balenciaga bag, or Western fashion brands. Shifting away from the question of intention, this chapter is concerned with issues related to the meme's impact and the possibilities of crowdsourced IP regulation when it's approached "from below." What effect does the meme, particularly social media users' appropriation of the Balenciaga hashtags, have on Balenciaga's brand name, brand image, and market share? In other words, I'm interested in the material and symbolic outcomes of Thai users' regulatory actions. To this end, we need to take a closer look at the meme, paying particular attention to the meme's appropriation of brand hashtags and what this appropriation enables and dis-enables.

But, first, a quick overview of what hashtags are. In their most basic form, hashtags are labels—usually keywords, names, and topics—that are preceded by a hash or pound symbol (#). Because hashtags are now hyperlinked (since 2009), clicking on any one tag enables users to see other public posts labeled with that hashtag. In this way, hashtags help to organize and make social media posts searchable. Beyond their practical functions, hashtags also have an important social networking function. They create metadata streams that users can follow to find more information and more discussions about specific topics. Sometimes this can lead to new perspectives and new connections. But as danah boyd has pointed out, hashtags *enable* these broader interactions but don't guarantee them. Hashtags can also limit and potentially close off one's online engagement to include only those who already share our interests, perspectives, and sensibilities.[8] Finally, hashtags have a rhetorical function that allows for metacommentary. Hashtags can inject humor, irony, sarcasm, or some other personal aside to a social media post that adds to or clarifies the main message.

Brand hashtags—hashtags that identify a brand by its name (e.g., #Nike) or by its slogan (e.g., #JustDoIt)—have several functions that act together to serve a company's commercial interests. One of these functions is citational. Companies use brand hashtags to market the brand and to promote the brand's products or services. In these instances, the hashtag is simply used to identify a product's or service's commercial source. Brand hashtags also have a semiotic function. Companies create online stories, images, and campaigns that imbue the brand hashtag with positive associations. Hashtags are used to cultivate brand appeal in terms of product quality, corporate values, and so on. The semiotic potential of brand hashtags, then, also makes them useful public relations tools. They help to expand brand recognition, consumer loyalty, and brand trust.

In 2010, companies began capitalizing the semiotic value of hashtags by characterizing them as intangible assets that generate "goodwill," a legal term for a brand's public reputation. Holding that goodwill is protectable as IP, companies—first in Europe and then in the United States—sought trademark protection for their hashtags.[9] They rationalized that trademark protection would enable them to strengthen their brand's goodwill by preventing others from trading on it. *Women's Wear Daily* reports that "clothing, footwear and headgear are the most common classification of goods and services with trademarked hashtags, with more than 800 so far."[10] As of this writing, the United States leads all other countries in hashtag trademark applications, followed at a distance by Brazil, France, the United Kingdom, and Italy. (In 2015, the United States filed 1,042 hashtag trademark applications while Brazil filed 321.[11] The gap between the two countries has shrunk since 2015 but the United States still holds a significant lead.)

Although hashtag trademarks are becoming more commonplace, not everyone agrees that hashtags should be trademarked. Robert T. Sherwin has pointed out that hashtag trademarks are oxymoronic by definition: hashtags encourage use by others while trademarks prohibit such use.[12] And companies *want* others to use their hashtags. For example, a common business practice is to encourage consumers to tag their personal social media posts with the brand hashtag as a condition of participating in a prize giveaway or as a way of declaring their membership in a brand community. These have become common consumer practices in the age of social media. Companies and consumers alike view hashtags as informal and fun ways to interact. But hashtag campaigns also foster a distinct understanding of and approach to labor under digital capitalism.

Fashion hashtag campaigns recruit internet users to engage in unpaid marketing work (by producing and distributing content) under the pretense of social interaction. In subtle ways that are now pervasive, fashion companies (along with the social media companies that own these platforms) are extracting value from social media users' content production while exerting greater control over the use and circulation of that content. With hashtag trademarks, companies are trying to have it both ways, to extract as well as constrict the productive resource of user-generated online content. As Sherwin observes, "The only reason for a company to trademark a word or phrase with an appended hashtag is to increase leverage over social media networks and users when the discussion goes south."[13] Hashtag trademarks aren't my main concern though, since the Balenciaga hashtag doesn't appear to be trademarked. I mention them because they help to illustrate the growing cultural and economic value of brand hashtags, a necessary context for understanding the significance of the Thai/Balenciaga meme and the regulatory action it performed.

In the Thai/Balenciaga meme, the Balenciaga brand hashtags function as the site, object, and means of struggle over the truthfulness of brand marketing. It's not an overstatement to say that the meme's viral popularity depended on the hashtags. Without them, the meme almost certainly would have remained an inside joke within Thailand. In an article about the Balenciaga show, an *Elle* journalist described accidentally finding the Thai meme "while cruising the #balenciaga hashtag earlier today."[14] As well as *Elle*, many other US and European media outlets, such as the *Telegraph*, the *Guardian*, British *Vogue*, *Cosmopolitan*, and *Mashable*, published stories that at least mentioned, if not featured, the meme. Whether journalists discovered the meme by "cruising" the hashtags themselves or through others who had cruised the hashtags before them, Western media outlets that reported on the meme unwittingly became free information brokers to Thai social media users—many of whom had a relatively small number of followers. In directing their vast audiences to the meme, *Elle*, *Vogue*, the *Guardian*, and the rest unintentionally amplified the meme's regulatory power. In a circular fashion, the media coverage helped spread the meme, which helped "trend" the hashtags, which attracted more audiences to the debates about the provenance of the Balenciaga tote bag, which further spread the meme, and so on.[15] What was intended to mark the debut of an exciting new fashion collection—the hashtag—became the site of and means for questioning the full novelty of that collection.

Thai social media users' memetic regulation follows in the tradition of culture jamming, a kind of consumer-based media action that co-opts corporate media platforms and channels in order to "jam" or trouble the smooth functioning of commercial activities. Mark Dery explains that the term is derived from "CB slang for the illegal practice of electronically interrupting radio broadcasts, conversations between fellow hams or the audio portions of television shows."[16] Likewise, culture jammers "introduce noise into the signal" of corporate messaging as a way of "intruding on the intruders" of public space.[17] These practices and their histories span a wide range of media sites and approaches, including the Situationist practice of detournement, or what a cofounder of *Adbusters* magazine, Kalle Lasn, defines as a "rerouting [of] spectacular images, environments, ambiences and events to reverse or subvert their meaning [and] thus [reclaim] them."[18] (This definition captures the specific mode of culture jamming that Thai users engaged in when they appropriated the Balenciaga hashtags.) Other tactics of culture jamming include the neo-Situationists' billboard banditry; mid-twentieth-century practices of ad-busting; various practices of "guerilla semiotics"; "semiotic Robin Hoodism"; "rhetorical jujitsu"; and an array of parody, gripe, and "suck" websites.[19] While the means and targets of culture jamming vary, a common thread that links these practices is an interest in and knack for commercial interruption, sabotage, and subversion.

The Thai/Balenciaga meme can be located within a more recent tradition of computer-based culture jamming. The history of Web 1.0, or the pre–social media internet, is filled with cases of consumer-generated culture jams. Rosemary J. Coombe and Andrew Herman's research is particularly salient here.[20] As they've demonstrated, much of the culture jamming that consumers engaged in during this period specifically targeted IP bullies, corporations that were known to use IP law as an instrument and rationale for censoring criticism. Early internet users pushed both the boundaries and the issue of trademark infringement. They created and circulated satirical brand names, logos, ads, and company websites "not simply to articulate a counterdiscourse," Coombe and Herman argue, "but to subvert the symbolic economy of the corporate persona as intellectual property."[21] In other words, these culture jams were themselves a kind of extralegal regulatory action.

The Thai/Balenciaga meme is a fashion trial by social media that operates like a culture jam. It relies on social media engagements and architectures to adjudicate some issue of fashion copycatting, with the effect of "jamming" up brand and industry marketing messages. But as I explain below, I don't see Thai social media users' hashtag jamming as interrupting Balenciaga's marketing so much as clarifying it. By co-opting brand hashtags and hashtag-based networks, Thai users are providing what Gvasalia and the Balenciaga company don't: honest product-source information. In this way, the Thai regulatory meme helps to realize what is an often-preached but rarely practiced ideal in the rhetoric of ethical fashion and corporate social responsibility: supply-chain transparency.

Reclaiming the Rainbow Bag by Any Meme Necessary

When the day began in Paris on March 6, 2016, the Balenciaga hashtag primarily referenced the brand's upcoming and highly anticipated marketing effort, a runway show introducing the Balenciaga Fall 2016 ready-to-wear collection at Paris Fashion Week. This was also the debut collection of its new head designer, Demna Gvasalia. By the end of the day, though, the Balenciaga hashtags had taken on new meanings and significance as Thai internet users tacked the Balenciaga hashtags to countless online photos of the Thai rainbow bags.

Thai news outlets credit the first iteration of the meme to actress Pattarida "Tangmo" Patcharaveerapong, who posted an Instagram photo of herself with a large rainbow bag on March 6 (the same day of the Balenciaga show).[22] Her Instagram account is now deactivated but her photo can still be seen online in news articles about the meme. Another early iteration of the meme appeared on the Facebook page of a user going by the name of Wise Man, or นักปราชญ์ (figure 3.1). Wise Man's Facebook post, also published on March 6, is composed of side-by-side photographs of himself and a Balenciaga model wearing nearly identical tote bags (in size, shape, and textile pattern).[23] He jokes in the status update of his Facebook post that (with his newly fashionable bag), he's "ready to strut to the [upscale] Siam Paragon mall #balenciaga #balenciagabag."[24] The Facebook post received 2,700 reactions and 89 comments and was shared 176 times. Nearly all of the comments riff on Wise Man's joke about the stylishness of the Thai bag. Some teased that early releases were already available at Pratunam, a popular and cheap outdoor market. (The Balenciaga version would not be released for six more months.) Many joked that the original Thai bag was the superior bag, pointing to its budget-friendly price and its "waterproof" construction (it's made of plastic rather than leather). Several users like Pond Chatchai Trirongrak and Natakhon Teerawornmongkhon took the copycatting more seriously. Trirongrak stated "Paris is always taking from Thailand and its neighbors" and Teerawornmongkhon openly speculated that the Balenciaga bags might constitute "a copyright issue."[25]

For more than a few days after the runway show ended, Thai social media users continued to create and share more iterations of the meme. Together, they reveal a wide range of reactions to the Balenciaga bag from bemusement to annoyance to anger. The vast majority of these social media posts did not include comparison pictures of the Paris show or the luxury bags. The most common iteration consisted of one photo featuring

FIGURE 3.1. Screenshot of Wise Man's Facebook post, March 6, 2016.

a Thai person or group of people and/or the Thai bags, annotated with at least one Balenciaga hashtag.

One example is Eric Tobua's Instagram post (figure 3.2). The post consists of a single photo of Tobua walking across the frame. An ivy wall is visible in the background. He's wearing a black leather jacket over a black T-shirt and black plaid pants. The rainbow bag on his shoulder is the brightest thing in the photo. The post's caption is only one word, written in the form of a question, "Balenciaga??"[26] Trailing the caption is a long string of hashtags, eleven lines deep. The first one is #balenciaga. Some of the other hashtags (they're all in English) are #samesamebutdifferent, #inspired, and #catchoftheday. Tobua is poking fun at Balenciaga but his culture jam is more like gentle teasing—the double question marks are emphatic but still playful. The ambiguity of his post may be why it was republished in articles that interpreted the meme in contradictory ways. For example, it appears in the *Cosmopolitan* article declaring that Thai social media users were LOVING the Balenciaga lookalike bags and it appears in an online magazine called *Runway Riot* where it was used to demonstrate that the Balenciaga bag "looked eerily familiar to popular shopping bags in Thailand"—the lookalike bag, this writer argues, is an added insult to the injury of Gvasalia's all-white runway show.[27]

Less ambiguous is an Instagram post created by a user named "p.m. orm" who is more clearly irritated with the brand.[28] Orm's Instagram photo is similar to Tobua's. She's dressed entirely in black and walking across the frame—this time, through an unidentified shopping mall (possibly Siam Paragon, the ritzy mall mentioned earlier). And, like Tobua's post, the most colorful item in the photo is the rainbow bag on her shoulder. Tobua's and Orm's photographs exemplify classic fashion blogger "snapshot aesthetics" (e.g., the in situ poses and the elsewhere gazes).[29] But, in this context, it's hard not to compare them to the images of the Balenciaga models walking across the runway, images in wide circulation at the time. The prominent placement of the Balenciaga hashtags also encourages this comparison. Tobua's post begins with the brand hashtag while Orm's begins and ends with them. Orm's entire caption consists of only two hashtags ("#balenciaga" and "#balenciagabag") and a single eye-roll emoji. In its curtness, Orm's iteration of the meme passes silent but unambiguous judgment against the luxury brand and its copycat bag.

erictobua

erictobua BALENCIAGA ??
#balenciaga #LOVES #love #loveit
#samesamebutdifferent #inspired
#inspiration #dope #style
#styleoftheday #streetstyle
#verystreetstyle #picoftheday
#pictureoftheday #photogram
#photograph #trend #fashiontrend
#instacool #instamood #instadaily
#instalove #colourful #colouroftheday
#mensfashion #menstyle #mensstyle
#cool #bestoftheday #catchoftheday

280w

whosyourdado Fab!

280w Reply

86 likes

MARCH 8, 2016

Add a comment...   Post

FIGURE 3.2. Screenshot of Eric Tobua's Instagram post, March 8, 2016.

At the time of this writing, Tobua's post still has only 85 likes and his follower count is just under 4,000. Orm's post has 57 likes and her follower count is 1,600. Although these are modest numbers in the context of social media influence, they're also misleading. They don't reflect how widely these and other images circulated through popular media outlets in stories covering the meme. (I already mentioned that Tobua's post appears in US *Cosmopolitan*; it also appears in the Hungary edition of *Cosmopolitan* and US *Elle*. Orm's post appears in *Mashable* and *Daily Mail*.) For more than a week—a significant amount of time in fashion terms—it was nearly impossible to read or see anything about the Balenciaga collection without also reading about and/or seeing the Thai/Balenciaga meme.

As popular as the meme was, though, it didn't "cancel" the Balenciaga brand or the lookalike bag. Social media users didn't call for a boycott of the brand, no one destroyed their Balenciaga products, retailers didn't pull Balenciaga stock from their shelves and inventory, and no public apology was demanded (or offered)—Gvasalia and Balenciaga were spared some of the most common costs that fashion brands tend to incur when they're on the receiving end of a viral social media trial. About two and a half years later in November 2018, Chinese social media users in China and the diaspora would exact all of these punishments from Dolce & Gabbana after Stefano Gabbana's anti-Asian rant was leaked to the public via Instagram.[30] But Thai social media users in general weren't accusing Balenciaga of racism (a more clear-cut offense that activates a wider set of critics in the diaspora and worldwide) and Thai consumers don't hold the same level of social, cultural, and purchasing power that Chinese consumers now wield.

In addition to Thailand's modest market power, a second reason Gvasalia/Balenciaga wasn't canceled has to do with the particular form of extralegal regulation Thai users were engaging in. Social media trials that are also culture jams function symbiotically with the brand they're passing judgment on. Culture jams operate by absorbing and refracting the brand's visibility by using its own hashtags. The hashtag meme worked because journalists and consumers were already following Balenciaga's hashtags. Memetic regulations are only as effective as the meme objects—the brand and the brand hashtags—are popular. "Canceling" the brand would have canceled the hashtag action.

Rather than cancel the Balenciaga hashtag conversation, Thai social media users redirected it toward a different conclusion. I want to emphasize that this redirection doesn't constitute an *interruption* of the Balenciaga hashtag conversation. Thai social media users weren't interrupting or intruding in a conversation that had nothing to do with them. By virtue of Balenciaga's copycatting, Thai people were already implicated in the conversation, whether Balenciaga acknowledged them or not. The meme enabled Thai people to participate in a conversation Balenciaga excluded them from. The meme expresses the other side of the hashtag conversation—the Thai side—shut out by Balenciaga's failure to cite its design source. In this sense, the meme kept the hashtag conversation and Balenciaga's marketing honest by making transparent the Thai source of the Balenciaga bags. What was intended to serve as an indicator of the bags' commercial origins became the object and means with which Thai social media users clarified the bags' origins and repositioned themselves as fashion and style originators.

Although I don't consider the Thai regulatory action to be an "interruption" to the Balenciaga hashtag conversation, the citational corrective it offered produced material effects that did intervene in Balenciaga's commercial activities. Recalling the words of the Malaysian journalist, Thai social media users' regulatory practices did in fact come at Balenciaga's expense. Let me explain.

Whether brand hashtags are corporate property or not, the branded product and event they reference are matters of significant material and nonmaterial investments. And when that branded event takes place on a global stage like a runway show at Paris Fashion Week, it involves vast amounts and types of expenses, such as the following:

- raw materials
- preshow labor (e.g., the designer and design firm, the cutters, sewers, trimmers, finishers, couriers, shippers, and runway set designers)
- venue fees (e.g., fees for renting the venue, the lighting, and the seats)
- on- and off-stage labor (e.g., models, hairstylists, makeup artists, caterers)
- transportation and lodging
- publicity and public relations (now defrayed but not entirely offset with social media)

The investments (and risks) are even greater when the show features a new designer's debut collection. As a result, an elite runway show like Balenciaga's can cost many hundreds of thousands of dollars. (Balenciaga doesn't disclose this information but as a relative comparison, the Marc Jacobs 2011 New York Fashion Week show lasted nine-and-a-half-minutes and cost "$1 million, or something like $1,750" per second.[31] And as staggering as that cost rate is, it is still only a fraction of the cost of more expensive events like a Victoria's Secret show.[32])

When Thai social media users redirected the hashtag conversation away from the Balenciaga bag to the Thai rainbow bag, they redirected some of the "payoff" of these investments (e.g., publicity and sales) away from Paris to Thailand. The regulatory action threw a wrench in the common presumption of cultural inspiration/appropriation. If, to invoke Turtle Mountain Chippewa scholar Jessica Metcalfe's formulation, cultural inspiration/ appropriation treats nonwhite cultures as a "free bin" of symbols, practices, and designs (free for the taking and for corporate profit making) then Thai users' crowdsourced regulation represents an instance in which a source community succeeds in exacting a cost from the brand doing the taking (whether the taking is defined as inspiration or appropriation).[33] This time, a brand's "racialized taking" isn't free.

As the previous chapters document, crowdsourced IP regulation tends to preserve dominant social and market hierarchies. Brands rely on social media users to maintain hegemonic relations of prestige and power by enforcing normative understandings of innovation or inspiration and imitation. The Thai/Balenciaga meme, though, redistributes the balance of prestige and power *by redistributing digital content*, now a vital means and source of capital accumulation. The Thai hashtag action redirects the uses and meanings of Balenciaga's brand content and communication channels so that they challenge the presumption and benefits of cultural inspiration/appropriation, racial entitlements rarely granted to nonwhite designers. The presumptions of cultural inspiration/appropriation, as racial entitlements, have shielded white designers from the material and symbolic costs that come with the accusations and stigma of being labeled a knockoff artist, pirate, or fake. In other words, the presumptions of cultural inspiration/appropriation serve as de facto, informal copy rights (two words). They provide some with the rights to copy, to benefit from copying, and to exclude others from the same privileges.

Today, social media interactions and architectures are key sites for the preservation and normalization of this de facto copy right, but, as the Thai/Balenciaga meme demonstrates, they also provide the means for refusing this entitlement to take and benefit from the "free bin." The Thai hashtag jam effectively draws payment (in the forms of attention and information capital) from Balenciaga for its unauthorized and uncredited use of the Thai design. At the same time, it increased the transparency of Balenciaga's supply-chain information.

But the hashtag action didn't just impact Balenciaga's brand reputation, trustworthiness, and digital marketing strategy: it also had an effect on the Thai rainbow bags. By redirecting the Balenciaga hashtag conversation from the Balenciaga tote bag to the Thai rainbow bag, social media users (and their unwitting accomplices in the fashion press) boosted consumer demand and sales. Consumers who didn't want to wait six months for the Balenciaga bag or pay thousands of dollars for it now had the necessary information to go straight to the source. The Thai bag's renewed popularity within and outside Thailand led to a 33 percent increase in the price of the bag from 75 baht to 100 baht, or $2.46 to $3.28.[34] That is to say, the meme activated a transfer of value from Paris to Bangkok, a reversal of the conventional direction of value flow in cases of cultural inspiration and appropriation. All of this happened on Balenciaga's dime.

Thai social media users' actions dimmed Gvasalia's spotlight and Balenciaga's integrity. It also helped to chip away at the myth of the racial binary that locates innovation in the West and imitation in Asia. On one hand, the meme placed the Balenciaga name within a new field of connotations associated with derivativeness, imitation, and dishonesty. On the other hand, the qualities of originality and fashion-forwardness the Balenciaga hashtag was meant to index were resignified with people and places stereotypically associated with copycatting, a lack of imagination, and developmentally lagging behind the fashion times. As a Thai Facebook user named Junpen Onoon facetiously put it, "This shows we are the world's fashion leaders."[35] Of course Onoon knows that one social media meme—even a viral one—doesn't have the power to overcome centuries of Orientalism and Western developmentalist thinking around inspiration/innovation and imitation. But the meme did help to uncover the racial and colonial politics that often get obscured by the mystifying language of ethical fashion.

The Afterlife of the Meme

My point isn't to romanticize the counterhegemonic work the meme did or the power of individual consumer actions. The meme didn't reverse or undo the inequalities structuring the relationship between fashion centers in the Global North and fashion peripheries in the Global South. It didn't balance out the unequal divisions of labor, benefits, and access to resources and privileges (such as the power to copy and/or control the use and meanings of cultural resources)—divisions that have resulted in a concentration of power and wealth for those living and working in the upper segments of the global-fashion supply chain and a concentration of precarity and poverty for those in the lower segments. Leveling these imbalances requires structural changes in international labor, trade, IP, and foreign investment policies, not individual consumer actions. The public responses to the meme, though, are reminders that the right to copy and the punishments for copying aren't equally distributed in the global fashion market. Cultural production doesn't take place on an even field of formal or informal IP ethics (e.g., copynorms), particularly when it comes to fashion.

Two things that happened after the meme went viral underscore the colonial character of international IP norms. First, Thai consumers began expressing concerns that, outside of Asia, the rainbow bag might be mistaken for a counterfeit Balenciaga bag and that they might be treated as fashion IP criminals. Recognizing their position in global fashion's racial order, they worried that being seen with the Thai bag—now that Balenciaga had copied it—would subject them to undue policing and, in places like Italy, cost them potentially thousands of dollars in fines. As the media coverage about these concerns grew, Thailand's head of intellectual property, Nantawan Sakuntanak, issued a public response. This was the second major thing to happen after the meme. In a strangely defensive press conference, Sakuntanak "assured the Balenciaga fashion house . . . that Thai-based handbag manufacturers have not broken intellectual property laws. Consumers could carry Thai-made handbags, which look similar to Balenciaga handbags, in Europe without concern."[36] She also added a second point of reassurance—again, addressed to Balenciaga—that the Thai government doesn't consider the Balenciaga bags a violation of copyright laws. "The Thai handbags are made of plastic and do not use leather like the Balenciaga handbags. They also differ in shape, colour, design pattern and trademark. So, neither the Thai-based bag manufacturer nor Balenciaga have legal standing to file a suit for violation of property rights."[37] This is an odd standard for judging fashion copies. Almost all fashion copies involve the use of different types and quality of materials and show variances in shape, color, and pattern from the original. Such differences are what brand experts and industry professionals teach consumers to look for when evaluating a product's authenticity. Whether the public chose to ignore or just missed Sakuntanak's racialized double standard, Western and Asian media outlets and social media users widely shared or paraphrased her statement as evidence used to vindicate Balenciaga and to undermine Thai consumers' regulatory actions as well as their concerns. While Thai consumers openly worried about being seen and treated in the West as fashion IP criminals, splashy media headlines definitively pronounced Balenciaga's innocence: "Balenciaga Did Not 'Copy' Traditional Thai Shopping Bags" (in the *Fashion Law* blog) and "Balenciaga's Market Bags Approved" (in *Vogue UK*).

In his lectures at the Collège de France (collected in the volume *Abnormal*), Michel Foucault argued that modern criminal justice systems are technologies for classifying individuals "who resemble their crime before they commit it."[38] Crowdsourced IP regulation demonstrates how informal systems of information and communication—social media—are also technologies for social regulation and reproduction. The copynormative assumptions and norms that locate Asians on the wrong side of the racial binary of innovation and imitation mean that Asians look like copycats whether they've made or are wearing copycat designs or not. They resemble the fashion crime before they commit it. If the right to copy and all the privileges it entails—the benefit of the doubt, sales, positive media coverage, and now a preemptive announcement from a foreign state official excusing the copycatting—is a racial privilege, then so too is the entitlement to call out fashion copying. The culturally constructed and socially enforced rights to copy, to not be copied, and to have one's accusations of copying be taken seriously are benefits that accrue to those who hold or can lay claim to the possession of whiteness.

Today, the Thai/Balenciaga meme is dead, but it has an afterlife in the #balenciagathailand hashtag. While the hashtag circulates within a number of social media platforms, its most prevalent use is on Instagram, where, as of this writing, more than 1.1 million posts are tagged with #balenciagathailand. It is by far the most popular #balenciaga[*country*] hashtag. As a comparison, #balenciagaitaly presently has 1,787 Instagram posts, #balenciagauk has 803 posts, #balenciagafrance has 758 posts, #balenciagausa has 511 posts, #balenciagacanada has 117 posts, and #balenciaganigeria has 10 posts. Clicking on any one of these hashtags, except for #balenciagathailand, will show Instagram posts that have something to do with a Balenciaga product (mostly shoes and handbags) or with fashion more broadly. In contrast, the vast majority of the #balenciagathailand posts reference something other than an actual Balenciaga product that may or may not be a copy. Some of the most popular brand names and items that appear in the #balenciagathailand hashtag stream are Comme des Garçons, Vetements, Adidas, Supreme, and the Thai rainbow bag.

In the #balenciagathailand hashtag, "Balenciaga" doesn't name a particular thing like a brand identity, brand image, or a store location. Instead, it names a locally constructed relationship to brand names and branding culture that is akin to the kinds of understandings and approaches to brand culture that others like Ackbar Abbas, Boatema Boateng, Brent Luvaas, Constantine V. Nakassis, Kedron Thomas, and Elizabeth Vann have written about in their work on cultural perceptions of branding and authenticity in China, Ghana, Indonesia, India, Guatemala, and Viet Nam, respectively.[39] In different ways and in different contexts, this body of scholarship describes what might be generalized as a Global South approach to branding and fashion that is less concerned with logos (i.e., private property) and more concerned with a garment's "looks" (i.e., its social meanings). A representative example is Nakassis's account of how Tamil fashion producers and consumers in Chennai, India, understand style: "Indeed, the local producers and consumers with whom I worked were rather indifferent to the brand: 'no one cares about brands' was a common refrain. . . . Rather, they were interested in clothing that looked like it was branded—that is, that had that 'look', as they put it—even as they were indifferent to actual brands and questions of brand authenticity more generally."[40]

In Guatemala, the Maya garment manufacturers, wholesalers, and consumers whom Thomas interviews in her book also prioritize branded looks over brands. In a discussion about *presentación*, "the way the garments will look to clients and, ultimately, to consumers," Thomas observes that although presentación "entails sewing labels into the collars of shirts and the waistbands of pants . . . there is often little attention paid to which brand name is used."[41] In other words, labels are important but the basis of their importance has little to do with trademark names and principles. Instead, they "are considered to be integral to the constitution of a particular look."[42]

In Viet Nam, the concept of a branded look is encapsulated by the term *kiểu* (in the style of). Like Mayan fashion producers and consumers, Vietnamese don't evaluate "mimic goods" or *hàng nhái*, against an international IP rights framework. As Vann explains, Vietnamese "conceive of the relationship between mimic and model goods as relational and hierarchical, rather than in terms of originality and uniqueness."[43] "Mimic goods" are hierarchically organized below "model goods" by virtue of being modeled and produced after them but they're not necessarily inferior—aesthetically, morally, or operationally—to the branded goods.

The indifference to brand authenticity doesn't reflect the fashion peripheries' cultural and moral underdevelopment. To the contrary, the indifference stems from a deep understanding of the racially and economically unequal geographies that globalization emerges from and sustains. Thai people's concerns about being racially profiled demonstrate a keen understanding of their location on the wrong side of the inspiration/imitation binary and that, within fashion centers, they are not seen as *authentic* fashion subjects. Such insights about the racial politics of the fashion ethical imaginary are typical across the Global South. As Thomas notes, a common topic in her conversations with Mayan fashion producers and consumers involved "the sociopolitical and geographical distances that separate Maya people who make and consume fashion from the places represented as the true sources of fashion in global marketing campaigns and official discourses, including in development narratives and antipiracy propaganda."[44] Mayan people—like Thai people—know they are both peripheral to and marginalized by global fashion systems even as they are centrally implicated in them.

The #balenciagathailand hashtag—another tactic of crowdsourced IP regulation—visualizes and stores in data form a Global South position to fashion IP in which illustrious brand names like "Balenciaga" are turned into floating signifiers constantly open to rearticulation and resignification from multiple local positions in the fashion periphery. In the #balenciagathailand hashtag, the Balenciaga name is linked to Thailand—in other words, an elite brand is linked to a fashion periphery—in a relationship that is constructed "from below," from a country that is situated in the lower segments of the globalized value chain as well as in the Global South. The #balenciagathailand hashtag defines the social value and meaning of commodities from this situated perspective rather than the universalist perspective of corporate marketing firms. In doing so, it references and carries on the spirit of the meme years after the meme has ended.

The Thai/Balenciaga meme and the #balenciagathailand hashtag point to a fundamental irony. These social media actions don't just put Balenciaga and what Luvaas terms "the regime of the global brand" on trial; they also challenge popular assumptions about Asians' negative or primitive relationship to technology.[45] Thai social media users' regulatory hashtag actions challenge the developmentalist stereotypes of Asians as culturally and ethically unsophisticated digital media users. While social media is dominated by commercial messages, Thai social media users demonstrate the possibility for innovative ways of creating other spaces within these corporatized media environments. Their hashtag actions are not quite anticommercial but they do make some headway against corporate fashion's business-as-usual racialized extractivism by pushing for more honest advertising and by taking and redistributing a significant share of a brand's attention capital and capital investments. Asians, widely associated with fake fashion and unethical internet behaviors, are here using social media in ways that facilitate the furtherance of not simply a more ethical but also more equitable global fashion market.

It may be that Junpen Onoon was right after all.

"Ppl Knocking Each Other Off Lol"

DIET PRADA'S POLITICS OF REFUSAL

The Instagram account called Diet Prada (@diet_prada) began as a joke, as silly banter between two coworkers and fellow fashion history buffs, Tony Liu and Lindsey Schuyler. As Liu tells it, "We would look at runway shows, just kind of shooting the shit, and we would do these live roasts back and forth sitting in opposite corners. One of us would pull up a show and say, 'Hey, look at this, it's so Louis Vuitton Fall 2014 . . .' We would just shoot comments back and forth."[1] In December 2014, Liu and Schuyler launched Diet Prada. The name pays tribute to the designer Miuccia Prada, "the original end-all be-all of everything," and to Diet Coke, "the original imitator."[2] The account's original and current "bio" simply reads, "Ppl knocking each other off lol." The pair ran the account anonymously for about two years until their identities were leaked online. At the time of this writing, Diet Prada has more than two million followers and nearly 1,200 unique posts—many of them generating thousands of user comments and tens of thousands of likes—and the account is a regular fixture in the media both as a subject and source of news.

Diet Prada's massive base of followers and its enormous influence make it an exceptional and instructive case of crowdsourced intellectual property (IP) regulation. (While Liu and Schuyler are responsible for creating the Diet Prada posts and framing the terms of engagement, Diet Prada is fundamentally a crowdsourced effort. Its posts would have little impact without the crowdsourced work its followers—and haters—do.)

Although no discussion of crowdsourced IP regulation would be complete without mentioning Diet Prada, it's impossible to write about it as if it's run and operates like other social media trials.

Liu and Schuyler are not ordinary social media users or fashion outsiders. They met while working in the fashion industry (doing design and product development for renowned milliner Eugenia Kim) and continue to work in the industry as a designer (Liu) and fashion consultant (Schuyler).[3] They also possess a virtuosic knowledge of fashion-design history, which enables them to draw more connections than the average consumer between designs across and within various time periods and market segments. Also, unlike most social media users whose participation in this kind of extralegal regulatory work is casual and irregular, Liu and Schuyler regard it and treat it *as* work. (Liu has described Diet Prada in terms of a business.[4]) They post new and increasingly thoughtful content on a frequent basis and although they don't make money directly from the content they produce (i.e., users don't pay to access Diet Prada's information), the site is an income-generating enterprise, thanks to a line of Diet Prada merchandise, a number of brand partnerships, and a Patreon subscription service.[5] Diet Prada marks the increasing professionalization of crowdsourced IP regulation. Whereas crowdsourced regulation is generally distributed across social media accounts and platforms, occurring spontaneously and sporadically in response to the latest copycat dispute, Diet Prada aggregates these activities and the online content they generate into one dedicated space.

To be clear, Diet Prada isn't the first website dedicated to exposing fashion copycats. Its predecessors include "Adventures in Copyright Infringement" (a regular column on the fashion news site *Fashionista*) and *Counterfeit Chic* (a blog run by law professor Susan Scafidi). But earlier sites largely transferred mass media techniques onto social media platforms. Although they used hyperlinked text and digital images, they took traditional journalistic forms like news articles and op-eds to call attention to fashion copycatting without *directly* calling out or prompting others to call out copycats.

Diet Prada is the largest and most centralized public archive of information and opinion about fashion copying. As such, it's a useful bellwether for assessing the shifting currents of crowdsourced IP regulation. In its extraordinariness, Diet Prada provides a future scenario example of the growing importance of social media as a site of value creation in the global fashion economy. While Diet Prada has fueled and continues to influence the rise of online fashion watchdogs, the most notable thing about the account is that it departs from or exceeds the mainstream parameters of this phenomenon in almost every way.

Diet Prada's use of native digital media practices and forms like screenshots, hashtags, GIFs, and memes as well as its hallmark side-by-side comparison post have not only helped to shape the development of crowdsourced IP regulation but also "localized" this work to Instagram. Before Diet Prada launched, Instagram was already fashion's favorite app for advertising and driving sales. But Diet Prada made Instagram into a key site for exposing the unfair labor and business practices that fashion ads on Instagram and elsewhere are designed to hide.

Following Diet Prada, there's been a proliferation of new Instagram accounts created for the express purpose of exposing copycats in fashion design, beauty, and other consumer-goods retail industries—evidencing, for many, the existence of a "Diet Prada effect."[6] The most commonly cited examples of this "effect" are the Instagram accounts Estee Laundry (focused on copycatting in the beauty industry), Diet Sabya (focused on copycatting in India's fashion-design industry), Retail Slam Book (focused on exposing bad corporate actors in "the retail scene"), and Diet Ignorant (a parody site created for the sole purpose of undermining Diet Prada's credibility). Ironically, Diet Ignorant may be the best evidence of the Diet Prada effect.

This effect is as much a myth as it is a reality though. There's no doubt that Diet Prada has been instrumental in developing and popularizing the function of the Instagram-specific online watchdog. Yet Diet Prada's effect on its successors is limited and inconsistent. More often than not, the copycat accounts only resemble Diet Prada superficially in tone and form but miss its most important methodological and conceptual lessons. A closer look at Diet Prada reveals how much its understanding of the fashion copycat problem differs from and, in some ways, opposes the Instagram watchdog culture it is credited (or blamed) with popularizing.

Diet Prada's Instagram posts can be grouped into three major categories: posts that expose a specific copycatting incident, posts that address a larger structural problem of the fashion industry, and posts that take an absurdist approach to calling out fashion copycatting. The posts in the first category—those that spotlight a specific copycatting case—are those most readily associated with Diet Prada. These posts typically involve side-by-side comparison photos of two or more lookalike fashion garments, accessories, or editorials. Almost always, these posts call out an industry elite for copying another industry elite (e.g., Diane von Furstenberg copying Schiaparelli, 3.1 Phillip Lim copying Céline, JW Anderson copying Bonnie Cashin, etc.). Alternately, the posts in the first category take industry elites to task for copying culturally distinctive designs belonging to Indigenous and racialized people in fashion peripheries such as Mexico, Ecuador, Nigeria, and India.

It's worth underscoring that Diet Prada's targets are primarily elite fashion brands, blue-chip designers, celebrity photographers, and peer social media "influencers" (e.g., Dolce & Gabbana, Virgil Abloh, Terry Richardson, Marcus Hyde, Bruce Weber, Kim Kardashian West, and Arielle Charnas). Its practice of "punching up" or "punching laterally" is the most striking but least-appreciated difference between Diet Prada and other online fashion watchdogs. Generally, internet fashion watchdogs—including the Instagram accounts that emulate Diet Prada—"punch down." They overwhelmingly target those who are less known and/or less powerful, exploiting and reaffirming social and market hierarchies. As earlier chapters in this book have shown, fashion trials by social media often employ the language of consumer and commercial ethics while shoring up existing power inequalities.

In one of the more egregious examples of "punching down," Estee Laundry (an anonymous, group-run account) posted Kanye West and Kim Kardashian West's Christmas family photo for the purposes of commenting on the appearance of the Wests' five-year-old daughter. The post's caption, which focuses on the girl's bright red lip gloss, is phrased in the form of a question: "Is it a bad idea to let a 5-year old think that she needs makeup and straight hair to be considered pretty, or is it just harmless fun? [Thinking Face emoji]."[7] Although the caption hints at a feminist discourse (do girls need makeup and straight hair to be pretty?), feminism here is a pretext for justifying its decision to make this little Black girl an object of public critique. (Kardashian West's parenting is indirectly but clearly a second object of critique.) Estee Laundry's post engages in what's known today as "concern trolling," an online act of harassment that's cloaked in the guise of concern or worry. Neologism aside, though, this kind of "punching down" isn't new or unique to social media. It mirrors much older racist and misogynist traditions of policing Black women's and girls' bodies and sexuality against the invisible yet pervasive standards of white, middle-class, feminine respectability.

The Estee Laundry post is instructive for several reasons. First, as I've already suggested, it illustrates how ethical consumer activism can inadvertently mobilize oppressive ideas and actions. Second, it evidences how race and gender continue to shape fashion and beauty economies even when the modes of production shift from industrial to informational, corporate-produced to crowdsourced, and vertically organized to decentralized and distributed. Finally, and most saliently for this discussion, it underscores Diet Prada's distinctiveness in relation to the phenomenon it helped foster. Liu and Schuyler don't follow the common practice of pinning industry problems on those with the least influence and power (e.g., budget brands, budget consumers, children) while absolving those with the most influence and power of their role in perpetuating these problems (e.g., elite brands and consumers). Diet Prada's copycatting posts, like its other posts, avoid many of the racist, gendered, and classist pitfalls that characterize so much of the mainstream discussions about ethical fashion. This isn't to say that Diet Prada entirely ignores budget brands. But only nineteen of its current total 1,183 posts, or 1.8 percent of its archive, mention a budget brand and half of these posts take a positive or neutral position toward that brand. The remaining 1,162 posts, or 98.2 percent of its archive, focus on an elite fashion brand or figure. (In the time it took me to complete this chapter, Diet Prada's archive of posts has steadily increased in number but the proportion between budget-brand posts and designer/elite-brand posts has remained remarkably stable at 1.7 to 1.9 percent.)

The second category of Diet Prada posts emphasizes the structural problems that pervade the global fashion industry, particularly racism, misogyny, sexual predation, and labor exploitation. And, again, its primary targets are elite designers, luxury fashion campaigns, celebrity photographers, and powerful media figures. These structurally focused posts are now as commonplace as those focusing on "ppl knocking each other off." And they may be more popular since they dare to name, shame, and, in some cases, *flame* industry giants. Here, I'm thinking about the Diet Prada video showing a pair of hands in black leather gloves setting fire to a Dolce & Gabbana label before flicking it out of frame. The video was widely understood as a response to Stefano Gabbana's repeated insistence of "I'm not gay, I'm a man." Many condemned his remarks as antigay and saw it as part of a longer history of Gabbana's internalized homophobia.[8] The video got nearly 200,000 views and 1,360 individual comments, many of them generating their own comment threads.

A third category of posts turns toward the absurd. Although they share the same formal qualities with the fashion copycatting posts (e.g., side-by-side comparison photos), their content undercuts the seriousness of the copycatting accusation and the seriousness of fashion policing more broadly. While fashion copycatting is generally viewed as a major problem in need of a major response ("a crime wave unprecedented in human history," in the completely unironic words of a 2013 documentary[9]), a significant number of Diet Prada's posts poke fun at fashion, fashion policing copycats, and fashion copycatting itself. Absurd comparisons between, say, Bottega Veneta's macramé-woven mule pumps (retail: $1,046) and a brick of instant ramen noodles (retail: 3 for $1.00) or posts juxtaposing other high fashion objects with mundane things like cured meats, dog snouts, pasta, and human intestines knock high fashion down several notches and poke fun at the high seriousness of anti-fashion copycatting efforts—including the Diet Prada project (more on this later).[10] It's this third category of posts where the mocking irony of Diet Prada's Instagram bio ("Ppl knocking each other off lol") is most clearly represented (figures 4.1 and 4.2).

Posts from the second and third categories—those that don't deal directly or seriously with fashion copycatting—tend to be read as outside of Diet Prada's regular program of fashion policing (i.e., "a break from calling out fashion phonies").[11] But such interpretations miss an important fact about the ecosystem of Instagram accounts and consequently miss Diet Prada's significance. Instagram posts are not standalone units. They're linked together systemically through data channels like name hashtags (e.g., #dietprada) and Instagram handles (e.g., @diet_prada) and they're linked conceptually under the rubric of the account's "bio." (Diet Prada's bio, "Ppl knocking each other off lol," has remained unaltered since its first post.) Thus, the posts that are *not* explicitly about fashion knockoffs are nonetheless structurally connected to those that *are*.

FIGURE 4.1. Screenshot of a Diet Prada post that compared a sausage to a Bottega Veneta shoe, September 6, 2019.

FIGURE 4.2. Screenshot of a Diet Prada post that compared a dog's snout to a Saint Laurent dress, September 25, 2019.

Liu and Schuyler's diverse archive of posts broadens the context for understanding fashion copycatting by linking it to other issues of ethical sourcing. Concerns about the fair, responsible, and respectful treatment of *things*—fashion designs—are connected to issues about the fair, responsible, and respectful treatment of people, such as Indigenous and ethnic source communities, fashion models, and racially marginalized consumers, who directly and indirectly, willingly and nonconsensually contribute to the development of global fashion brands. This is the real difference between Diet Prada and other internet fashion watchdogs: its approach expands the interpretation and discussion of fashion copycatting into social and political domains.

On Diet Prada, posts about fashion racism, model abuse, Native appropriation, and so on are not external but integral to its primary focus.[12] They mark out the broader field of power in which Liu and Schuyler are defining and assessing the problem of "ppl knocking each other off." Diet Prada's framing of the copycatting problem strips away fashion's false neutrality, the notion that fashion is outside of or transcends politics—a popular sentiment captured in Karl Lagerfeld's much-quoted 2017 statement that "fashion people are fashion, they are not politics."[13] At a time when statements like Lagerfeld's are as commonplace as they are uncritical, Diet Prada is refusing to be neutral. Its posts refuse to normalize the power inequalities that condition the production of fashion design, fashion garments, fashion imagery, and, now, ethical fashion discourse.

The vast majority of media coverage and information about Diet Prada largely misses the political dimensions of its critiques. Instead, accusations of bullying and, conversely, of selective criticism (of going easy on their favorite brands) dominate the public discussions about the online fashion watchdog. Both interpretations are at best misleading and at worst dishonest. (If favorites like Miuccia Prada and Demna Gvasalia have been spared anything, it's Diet Prada's snark, not its criticism.[14]) Yet such accusations are symptomatic of the false equivalency and depoliticized discourse that pervade the mainstream thinking about fashion ethics. To understand Diet Prada's critiques of fashion elites as "bullying" is to interpret them in a political vacuum isolated from the matrices of racism, sexism, colonialism, and capitalism that structure the global fashion economy and underpin elites' privileged status within that economy. "Punching up" at the powerful isn't bullying. It's an act of refusing to normalize their power.

As we've seen throughout this book, elite designers and brands are typically exempt from the kinds and degrees of public scrutiny directed at budget brands and at nonelite fashion producers. Entrenched cultural and class fictions like copynorms that valorize elite forms of fashion copying as "inspiration," "appreciation," and "homage" and devalue nonelite forms of copying as "knocking off," "laziness," and "stealing" have historically operated to deflect criticism away from fashion elites and onto nonelites. Such fictions give rise and legitimacy to an array of lucrative benefits that flow to fashion elites and are denied to others. These include, as I've been arguing throughout this book, nonlegal but no less powerful "copy rights" or the right to copy with impunity (or with little cost), the right to not be copied, and the right to the benefit of doubt in court trials and social media trials about fashion copying. Diet Prada does not recognize or protect these copy rights.

Liu and Schuyler's regulatory practices are a lot like the Thai example of crowdsourced IP regulation discussed in chapter 3. Both groups are engaging in a kind of media-based consumer activism that co-opts a brand's media images, messages, and hashtags to expose the unfair labor and business practices hidden behind its slick branding strategies. Ironically, their counterhegemonic regulatory work helps to advance a primary goal of the corporate social responsibility mantra—to enhance the level of supply-chain transparency. I think of Diet Prada and the Thai social media users as doing this informal accountability work from opposite ends—the Thai users from the bottom up and Liu and Schuyler from the top down. Their disparate positions matter for understanding Diet Prada's impact and limits.

Diet Prada's high stature in the contemporary fashion-media landscape can be attributed, in part, to Liu and Schuyler's talents, but their individual actions and expertise alone are not enough to explain Diet Prada's success. Liu and Schuyler (and, subsequently, Diet Prada) benefit from structural advantages derived from their positioning within the Western hegemonies of global fashion, global media, and global capitalism—the very structures that disadvantage marginalized social media users and brands in fashion-market and fashion-media peripheries as well as in legal and social media trials of fashion copying. Liu and Schuyler's insider position in New York City and in New York City's fashion industry, that is to say, their insider location in a major cultural and economic center for fashion, gives them access to fashion shows, collections, social and professional networks, and gossip that Thai social media users and, indeed, most social media users don't have. Diet Prada's power to influence market dynamics and outcomes is thus a function of its structurally advantaged position. This isn't to take away from Diet Prada's achievements but rather to contextualize them. The context also underscores the structural barriers that social media users in fashion peripheries like Thailand or marginalized users in fashion centers face when they engage in crowdsourced IP regulation. Not all social media outrage is equal.

If Diet Prada can now be regarded as a global media brand, which I believe it can, then it's because it has absorbed and mastered some of the characteristics and practices of the elite corporate-fashion culture it's critiquing. Evidence of Diet Prada's designer features can be found in its line of branded merchandise; its signature look, voice, and feel; its branded hashtag "label" attached to every post; and its sloganesque Instagram bio. Diet Prada is a designer social media trial that trades on "designer dirt" (to borrow Naomi Klein's wonderfully apt term).[15]

Diet Prada's distinctiveness derives from the contradictory nature of its position and perspective. It's a fashion insider that uses insider branding strategies and forms to articulate an outsider cultural political discourse about the inequalities sustaining the global industry of which it's now a significant part. In doing so, Liu and Schuyler are using their power to challenge the global fashion-industry system. The absurd posts—as silly as they are—may be their most subversive posts. By heightening the absurdity of fashion copycat callouts, these posts undermine the very trend that gives Diet Prada its privileged place in social media and fashion-media landscapes.

The Diet Prada Value System

Like all consumers engaging in crowdsourced IP regulation, Liu and Schuyler's production and transmission of ethical fashion discourse is work that generates consumer and commodity values. As such, Diet Prada is a site of ethical and economic value creation. These value systems are intertwined. Dominant cultural definitions of creativity and ethics—what counts as inspiration or imitation, an ethical copy or unethical copy—animate market dynamics. Diet Prada's distinction from the mainstream of online fashion watchdogs is that it refuses the corporate neoliberal value system in which fashion ethics, fairness, and justice are defined in economic and property terms (e.g., loss of sales, brand devaluation, and cultural and market appreciation in which Western copies of ethnic and Native designs are rationalized as "appreciating" or "elevating" the source design's aesthetic and commercial value).[16] Diet Prada's judgments of fashion copying are guided by an alternative value system that refuses copynormative frameworks, logics, and shallow niceties.

My analysis of Diet Prada's politics and practices of refusal is informed by political anthropologist Audra Simpson's concept of refusal as a refusal to consent to hegemonic ways and structures of knowing and knowledge production. Refusal, Simpson explains, is a "deliberate" and "willful" "aware[ness] of [the] context of articulation" or of the broader conditions that structure meaning making.[17] A critical practice of refusal recognizes that the production and transmission of knowledge/information are deeply political processes embedded in, and constitutive of, unequal power relations. "Let's not pretend that there is an even playing field for interpretation," Simpson writes. "Let's not pretend that the Iroquois are not already prefigured, that their actions are going to be interpreted fairly."[18] The context of the "the settler-colonial present," she writes, makes for a "deeply unequal scene of articulation."[19] The epistemological legacy of settler colonialism delimits what is possible to know about Native people.

Rather than *resist* settler-colonial frames and modalities of meaning making—an oppositional position that, as Simpson points out, inadvertently "overinscribe[s] the state with its power to determine what matter[s]"—Simpson *refuses* them.[20] This isn't a negative critical practice but an affirmative one. Refusal "offer[s]," Simpson writes, "its own structure of apprehension."[21] Refusal advances a different way of knowing that begins from the recognition that the field of knowledge production and exchange is structurally tilted to favor settler-colonialist worldviews.

Diet Prada's politics and practices of refusal also advance a different way of understanding the problem of fashion knockoffs based on a deliberate awareness of the context of its articulation—a context marked by cultural, social, material, and geopolitical inequalities. That is to say, Diet Prada's refusal to confine its commentary about "ppl knocking each other off" *only to incidences of people knocking each other off* is a refusal to understand the problem of fashion copying within the dominant, economics-based US corporate framework of IP rights—as the loss of sales, of income, and of investments in brand equity. Diet Prada's approach to the problem of "ppl knocking each other off" assumes a different, more capacious—but not perfect—framework of values that includes concerns about the culturally and socially exploitative aspects of the fashion industry and that forges relations between those who are more vulnerable to fashion's many extractive processes. In this way, Diet Prada's refusal of fashion's dominant value system is an alternate practice of value and *values* creation, of constructing a set of consumer and commodity values that accounts for and is an accounting of power inequalities. (Diet Prada's politics may be influenced by the fact that Liu's mom worked, for a time, as a garment worker in an apparel factory in New York City. Liu seldom discusses his identity as an Asian American man or the ways that being a child of an Asian immigrant garment worker shape the work he does on and through Diet Prada, but it's reasonable to expect that this history informs the perspectives that characterize Diet Prada's posts.[22])

We can see Diet Prada's value system at work across its diverse collection of posts. I consider three very different cases. The first is a post that calls out the giant US retailer Target for selling a graphic T-shirt that prominently features—without credit or compensation—a copy of queer Mexican artist Felix d'Eon's painting of the gay pride flag, rendered as a Loteria game card. The second is a post calling out the Italian fashion house Maison Valentino for working with photographer and known sexual predator Terry Richardson on its Resort 2018 ad campaign. Lastly, I'll discuss what has become Diet Prada's most famous post—the one composed of a series of screenshots of Stefano Gabbana's racist remarks about China and Chinese people. Each of these posts articulates distinct concerns: racial extractivism, model abuse, and fashion racism. But what binds them together is the issue of ethical sourcing.

Ethical sourcing refers to a company's ethical conduct with regard to the many activities along its supply chain from resource procurement to production to distribution. Typically, ethical sourcing is measured by the impact that supply-chain activities have on the natural environment. Increasingly, ethical sourcing also considers the health and safety of workers who perform lower-end and lower-valued supply-chain activities (e.g., farmers, weavers, and garment workers). Diet Prada's conceptual parameters for ethical fashion sourcing are more expansive. It considers the *ethical* practices of designers, brands, and retailers as sources of social, cultural, and economic capital. The posts I discuss below provide multiple views of Diet Prada's value system and the role it's playing in influencing the performance of fashion supply chains and markets.

Target's Pride on Trial

The Target/d'Eon post appeared on May 15, 2018 (figure 4.3).[23] It consisted of side-by-side comparison photos of d'Eon's painting on the left and Target's T-shirt featuring d'Eon's artwork on the right. In d'Eon's painting, the gay pride flag is made into a Mexican Loteria game card, complete with card number and card title ("La Bandera"). D'Eon's full name also appears in a scroll that he placed between "La Bandera" and the flag it references. Target's copycat version replaces "La Bandera" with "Igualdad" (without the definite article—el or la—that conventionally precedes Spanish nouns and Loteria card names) and omits the scroll with d'Eon's name entirely. Target's T-shirt, priced at $12.99, was introduced as part of its Pride collection and was featured in its stores and websites in anticipation of the following month's Pride events. (June is Pride Month in the United States.)

In its post, Diet Prada points out the irony of Target's much-publicized support of queer communities and rights (with its offering of queer-themed products) and the dubious sourcing of at least one of its queer-themed products: "but are you really supporting those communities when you're stealing their original artwork?"[24] Implicit in this rhetorical question are several accusations involving Target's corporate hypocrisy, its unauthorized copying of a marginalized designer's artwork for its already-bloated coffers (in 2018, Target's revenue exceeded $75 billion), and its blatant capitalization of progressive politics for its own gain and at the expense of d'Eon's identity and relationship to the T-shirt's artwork.[25]

FIGURE 4.3. Screenshot of the Diet Prada post about Felix d'Eon and the Target knockoff, May 15, 2018.

The Target shirt literally erases d'Eon's name from the work he created and the ad symbolically whitewashes the painting's queer Mexican context with the image of a white male model named Brandon Lipchik.[26] (Diet Prada doesn't identify Lipchik. We learn his name because several readers commenting on the post tagged Lipchik while congratulating him for landing the Target ad.)

The Target/d'Eon post, like most of Diet Prada's posts, went viral. Almost immediately, it generated high levels of attention in the form of likes, comments, and shares. (At present, the post has 9,488 likes, 394 individual comments, and a significant number of comment responses.) Comments to the Target/d'Eon post fell within a familiar range of social media reactions, such as the following:

- reactive outrage ("Not ever buying there anymore" and "@target cut @felixdeon the damn cheque already!")
- reasoned outrage ("Instead of pulling why not give a portion of proceeds to the original artist and another portion to an LGBTQ organization? What happens to the clothing they pull. Not the most sustainable option.")

- glib contrarianism ("Bitch I need this shirt I'm Gay so might as well [followed by a series of different colored heart emojis]")
- casually racist, sexist, classist, and/or homophobic defensiveness ("Target has been one of the first major chains to openly support transgender people, but nooo . . . let's all shit on them bc they didn't hire *some street artist* to do work for them" (my emphasis)
- non sequiturs ("thank you for calling out @madewell for their blatant use of @citiesindust design")

And then there was Target's comment (discussed below).

Typically, brands avoid jumping into the social media fray especially when they're at the center of the fray, not because they're unaware it exists (impossible, given the widespread use of hashtags and user tagging) but because they know doing so will only prolong and possibly intensify the negative social media attention to their brand. But Diet Prada isn't a typical internet fashion watchdog site. While some designers have admitted that they're "scared of the social media army at Diet Prada's command," Diet Prada has become such a media juggernaut that *not* engaging comes with its own risks.[27] Brands risk appearing to Diet Prada's more than two million followers as out of touch with the digital fashion culture that Diet Prada signifies. They also risk appearing to the media outlets that now source their fashion news from Diet Prada as indifferent, or worse, callous to the ethical charges against them.

It's a tricky task but, more and more, designers including Stefano Gabbana, Diane von Furstenberg, and Christian Siriano are directly responding to Diet Prada's accusations *on the Diet Prada site*—a tacit acknowledgment of Diet Prada's influence as a regulatory mechanism for monitoring the fashion market. Of these three designers, only Siriano responded nondefensively to Diet Prada and immediately removed the copycat garment from his collection. His Instagram comment was brief and to the point: "Yea wow last time I have this designer in my studio make a dress. Agree, it's pulled."[28] Siriano's succinct response was largely applauded by Diet Prada followers and the media for being respectful and responsible. This is the kind of best-case scenario that designers imagine when they choose to respond directly to Diet Prada's accusations. The goal is to defuse the scandal by demonstrating a genuine willingness to face up to the charges and to speak directly to the social media judge and jury rather than hide behind PR platitudes and legal maneuvers. Instead of issuing carefully crafted press releases, more designers are opting to communicate directly with consumers by posting an (apparently) off-the-cuff and candid comment on Diet Prada or posting a response to Diet Prada on their own social media channels. These moves reflect fashion's changing public relations landscape, an industrial reality that Diet Prada helped bring about.

In contrast to Siriano, Target responded to the Diet Prada post in the more conventional language of corporate communications.

> @diet_prada Target respects the design rights of others and expects our vendors to do the same. We've pulled this shirt from Target.com and are addressing the issue with our vendor today. We spent a lot of time curating Pride merchandise that celebrates the LGBTQ+ and ally community and we apologize. We appreciate you bringing this to our attention.[29]

(The company provided virtually the same statement to media outlets covering the Diet Prada allegation.[30]) Target's statement manages to both deny and accept responsibility. It passes the blame down the supply chain to an unspecified vendor while paying lip service to the principle of corporate social responsibility (e.g., "addressing this issue with our vendor" and "we appreciate you bringing this to our attention").

Unsatisfied with its vague, stock response, Diet Prada and its followers challenged the company to commit to concrete actions that would provide restitution to d'Eon: "@target will you ensure @felixdeon is compensated for the number of units sold? How will the remaining products featuring his design be disposed of?"; "@target you need to pay @felixdeon even though it's been taken down. This is not okay!"; and "Ya le pagaron a @felixdeon por su diseño? Ya tienen un contrato por regalías????" (Have you already paid @felixdeon for your design? Do you already have a royalty contract????) And from the Diet Prada creators: "@target will you be pulling it from the physical stores as well?" Target never responded to any of these questions.

Diet Prada's post may not have gotten the desired reaction or restitution from Target but it nonetheless exacted a cost from the corporation. Symbolically, the T-shirt's bad publicity diminished Target's brand image with queer and queer-allied consumers at a crucial time just weeks before Pride Month. Financially, the T-shirt's subsequent removal from the Target website cost the company in terms of online sales, associated labor hours related to pulling unsellable inventory from shelves and moving them to storage facilities, and increased storage and insurance fees for dead stock. But Target's losses were d'Eon's gain in new fans and increased sales. The Diet Prada post reportedly boosted sales for d'Eon's Etsy shop where posters of his painting are still available for $60.[31] This exemplifies the uniquely redistributive character of Diet Prada's fashion trial by social media. Not only does Diet Prada's extralegal regulatory work refuse Target's racial extractivism, it uses the extractive event as an occasion and means for diverting publicity and money away from the corporate giant back to the queer Mexican artist whose cultural forms and heritage were being mined and marketed.

Maison Valentino, Boycott Terry

Another example of Diet Prada's more capacious approach to the concept of ethical fashion can be seen in its post condemning Maison Valentino's decision to work with photographer Terry Richardson on its Resort 2018 collection. This post demonstrates Diet Prada's concern for not only a brand's ethical treatment of things (e.g., designs) but also its ethical treatment of vulnerable supply-chain workers—here, fashion models.

On October 23, 2017, Diet Prada posted an ad from Valentino's Resort 2018 campaign, which it edited to include the words "Boycott Terry" in large block letters covering the entire image (figure 4.4). The post's caption questions the luxury brand's ethics: "You were well aware of Terry's reputation as a sexual predator, so why did you subject 7 women to this shoot and shamelessly promote the collaboration for your #valentinoresort2018 campaign? Is there no other talent in the industry you can work with?"[32] Diet Prada readers responded immediately to the post with positive reactions and supportive comments (e.g., "Finalllllyyyyyyyyyy oh my gawd"). But reactions to the post weren't limited to Diet Prada followers or to its Instagram page. An outpouring of leaked corporate documents, press releases, and media coverage followed the post's publication as well.

FIGURE 4.4. Screenshot of the Diet Prada post about boycotting Terry Richardson, October 23, 2017.

Within the first forty-eight hours of Diet Prada's post, a succession of major fashion-design and fashion-media companies publicly announced they would be cutting ties with Richardson (a calculated move designed—at least in part—to avoid ending up in Diet Prada's crosshairs). The first major announcement came from Condé Nast International, the giant media conglomerate that publishes, among other magazines, *Vogue, Glamour, W,* and *Vanity Fair.* In an internal email that was leaked the same day of the Diet Prada post, Condé Nast COO James Woolhouse announced that the company would no longer work with Richardson and that "any shoots that have been commission[ed] or any shoots that have been completed but not yet published, should be killed and substituted with other material . . . effective immediately."[33] The next company to renounce Richardson was Hearst Magazines (which publishes *Elle, Harper's Bazaar, Marie Claire,* and other titles). Soon after, Bulgari, Valentino, Prabal Gurung, and Diesel all promised to cut ties with Richardson.[34]

The domino reaction Diet Prada started reverberated across consumer and media channels. Readers gleefully shared news about Richardson's fall from industry favor on their own social media accounts and on Diet Prada's page, many posting congratulatory comments directly on the Valentino post ("THIS IS HAPPENING TOO FAST YOU GUYS SO PROUD"; "It's happening!! Well done, Diet Prada"; "You did it @ diet_prada!!! Terry Richardson and Valentino are no more! Awesome work"). Readers also posted names of more talented, more respectful, and mostly female photographers to hire instead of Richardson. Here, again, we see how Diet Prada's counterhegemonic regulatory work has redistributive effects. Its post reroutes what is a dominant extractive industry practice (e.g., celebrity fashion photographers using their gender and class power to exploit and profit from the professional and social vulnerability of fashion models) toward more inclusive ends. Diet Prada's post increased public demand to protect models and to hire more female photographers. In addition, it sparked a wave of media coverage about Richardson, the fashion industry's larger history of misogyny, model abuse, and the need for a #MeToo reckoning in the fashion industry.

As some readers rightly noted in their comments to the Diet Prada post, "it totally feels too little too late." By the time Diet Prada called out Valentino, budget brands like H&M, Target, and Aldo had already ended their relationship with the abusive photographer some three years earlier. Upscale fashion brands and magazines, though, continued to work with and defend Richardson years after his abusive behavior was public knowledge—until the Diet Prada post. This is not to suggest that Diet Prada solved the industry's model-abuse problem. Richardson continues to enjoy widespread support. In April 2019, US designer Tom Ford defended Richardson in the *New York Times* while blaming a "hyper-politically correct culture."[35] Richardson's Instagram account also remains active and popular. Among his one million followers are top brands like *Harper's Bazaar* magazine and the French clothing brand A.P.C.

Diet Prada's posts do not themselves transform the oppressive culture of the fashion industry, but they do have a cultural and material impact on upstream supply-chain activities where brand image is most visibly produced. The Diet Prada post forced Valentino, "the world's fastest-growing major luxury holding company" (with sales in 2017 topping

$1 billion), to listen, respond, and change course in less than twenty-four hours—as well as prompted a host of other major fashion institutions to do the same.[36] As well as diminishing Richardson's work opportunities and bank account, the Diet Prada post made Richardson, his work practice, and his hypersexualized aesthetic less cool (even if temporarily). That is to say, it helped to accelerate what Adbusters co-founder Kalle Lasn calls a bottom-up rebranding process of "demarketing" in which exploitative brands are rendered "uncool" and unappealing.[37] Today, the choice to work with Richardson remains, at best, a PR risk and, at worst, a PR nightmare for companies and celebrities. And with subsequent Diet Prada posts calling out other predatory photographers like Marcus Hyde (on July 22, 2019), Timur Emek (on July 23, 2019), Mario Testino (on November 24, 2019), and Bruce Weber (in an Instagram Story)—the MeToo movement may be finally coming into its fashion moment.[38]

The Fall of the "Great Show"

So far, we've seen how Diet Prada's approach to "ppl knocking each other off" includes considerations of how brands treat marginalized people's designs and how they treat one group of vulnerable fashion workers. In this section, we'll see how Diet Prada's value system includes a consideration of how brands treat racialized people.

On November 18, 2018, the Italian luxury brand Dolce & Gabbana released a series of videos in which a Chinese woman is being instructed on how to eat various Italian foods with chopsticks. As soon as the videos were released, Chinese social media networks lit up with angry posts about the Italian brand's presumption that it could teach Chinese people anything about using chopsticks and about the videos' portrayal of Chinese people as so unworldly that they would not know how to eat popular Italian foods like pizza, spaghetti, and cannoli. The videos were part of the brand's #DGLovesChina fashion campaign and were produced to generate hype for its "Great Show," an extravagant fashion show scheduled to be held in Shanghai. Reportedly, the brand was preparing to show five hundred looks.

Two days later on November 20, Diet Prada posted a series of screenshots of a heated exchange between Dolce & Gabbana designer Stefano Gabbana and model Michaela Phuong Thanh Tranova. Using Instagram's direct-messaging platform, Tranova expressed her objections to the brand's latest marketing efforts, objections that echoed sentiments already prevalent in Chinese social media sites.[39] But what Tranova and many others saw as a racist portrayal of Chinese people and Chinese culture, Gabbana insisted was "a tribute" that could only be misunderstood by people who "feel inferior." Finally exasperated by Tranova's persistent criticisms, Gabbana unleashed a diatribe of racist words and emojis about China and Chinese people including "Ignorant Dirty Smelling Mafia," dog eaters, and the shit emoji. (Tranova is ethnically Vietnamese.) Tranova responded by publishing the exchange on her own Instagram feed and, soon after, Diet Prada posted screenshots of Tranova's posts on its Instagram feed—an act that would bring the controversy to a new head (figure 4.5).

If the Orientalist videos weren't enough to contradict the brand's hashtag claim that #DGLovesChina, then the screenshots of Gabbana's racist invectives did the trick. As Diet Prada's screenshots went viral, a surge of social media outrage and press coverage followed. Many pointed out the contradiction between Gabbana's racist views of Chinese people

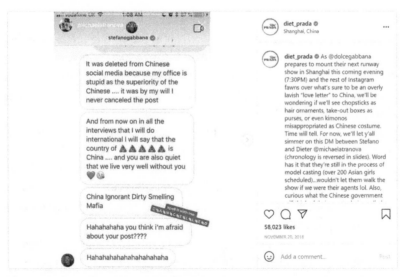

FIGURE 4.5. Screenshot of Diet Prada's post that displayed Stefano Gabbana's racist messages, November 20, 2018.

and his brand's efforts to attract the Chinese market. Today, the Diet Prada screenshots are widely credited with fomenting an international consumer, media, and retail backlash against the Italian luxury brand that, one year later (at the time of this writing), it still hasn't recovered from.

The first obvious signs of the backlash came minutes after Diet Prada's screenshots were published. Chinese models rehearsing for Dolce & Gabbana's "Great Show" began dropping out of the show—an action that Diet Prada suggested in the caption to its post.[40] One of the 350 models scheduled to walk in the show describes witnessing "bookers for the Chinese models . . . turning up and shepherding their models out" in the middle of dress rehearsal.[41] Meanwhile, the remaining models, she recalls, were "looking at @diet_prada, desperately trying to connect VPNs [virtual private networks] to cross-check what they're seeing against Stefano's Instagram, dissecting timelines and trying to work out whether or not he actually sent that message."[42] (Gabbana initially lied about his Instagram account being hacked.) Fewer than twenty-four hours after Diet Prada's post appeared and "a mere four hours before [the "Great Show"] was scheduled to begin," Dolce & Gabbana announced it was canceling the show. Of course, Diet Prada documented the cancellation with an Instagram post (figure 4.6).

The fallout worsened beyond and after the "Great Show." Chinese consumers—a market that "account[s] for at least a third of luxury sales and two-thirds of the industry's growth"—announced a boycott of Dolce & Gabbana products.[43] To underscore their seriousness, some consumers torched the products they already owned. Videos of Chinese consumers setting fire to Dolce & Gabbana products circulated swiftly throughout Chinese social media platforms. (These videos recall and perhaps were inspired by the video Diet Prada created earlier that year, in which someone in leather gloves burned a Dolce & Gabbana label.) Further, Chinese social media users had rebranded the Italian label as Dead & Gone, complete with a parody logo that circulated widely throughout Chinese social media networks.

In the retail sector, prominent Chinese e-commerce sites and luxury department stores, including Tmall, Taobao, JD.com, NetEase, Vipshop, and Lane Crawford, pulled the brand's products from their shelves. US and European retailers Sephora, Yoox, and Net-a-porter discontinued

FIGURE 4.6. Screenshot of the Diet Prada post about the Great Show being canceled, November 21, 2018.

selling Dolce & Gabbana products from their Chinese stores and Chinese platforms. International and local fashion magazines, including *Vogue China*, stopped running the brand's ads and stopped sending representatives to its shows. Two months after the Diet Prada post, the business news site *Bloomberg* observed that Dolce & Gabbana's gowns were noticeably absent at the Golden Globes and Oscars awards shows ("no A-lister dared to risk alienating fans by donning the label").[44]

In June 2019, about six months after the Diet Prada screenshots, the *New York Times* pronounced "the resurrection of Dolce & Gabbana."[45] But as Diet Prada immediately countered, white North American and European celebrities may have forgiven Gabbana but Chinese people—an increasingly significant luxury-market segment—had not: "So, whose reality does the NYT article actually depict? Friedman [the journalist] more or less writes the typical white-centric narrative around an issue that's actually global. Go figure . . ."[46]

It's impossible to know exactly how much in actual profits Diet Prada's post cost the Italian brand. According to one estimate by a London-based brand-valuation consultancy firm, "the scandal could wipe up to 20 percent," or $187.4 million, of "the Dolce & Gabbana brand's value of

$937 million."[47] But a defamation lawsuit against Liu and Schuyler—filed in 2019 and made public in 2021 on the Diet Prada site—suggests the luxury brand has a higher regard for the Instagrammers' influence than market consultants. Dolce & Gabbana's lawsuit seeks damages totaling more than $600 million to recuperate the brand's and Gabbana's images, the cost of the Shanghai show, and the loss of Asian sales.[48] At the time of this writing, the lawsuit is still pending. Also still pending is what the lawsuit *itself* will cost Dolce & Gabbana in sales and reputation. If the reaction to Diet Prada's post about the lawsuit and its plan to fight it is any indication though, the lawsuit will only make a bad situation worse for the Italian brand. Within its first thirty minutes, the Diet Prada post received more than 23,000 likes and nearly 700 comments—almost unanimously supportive.[49]

As the examples above demonstrate, Diet Prada frames the problem of "ppl knocking each other off" as a problem not simply of property relations but of unequal power relations. By situating the problem of fashion copying in relation to issues like model abuse and racism (generally considered to be outside the scope of the fashion copying problem), it highlights the larger political economy of fashion ethics. To use Audra Simpson's formulation, Diet Prada draws attention to fashion ethics' "context of articulation," a context structured by unequal industrial, media, and social power. Diet Prada's informal regulatory work increases the transparency of the global fashion-supply chain, expanding how we see and think about what ethical supply-chain activities and effects should look like.

Since the global spread of COVID-19, Diet Prada's attention has turned increasingly to reporting on the pandemic and the many socioeconomic inequalities it has exposed and exacerbated. In the early months of the pandemic, between March 2 and July 5, 2020, only ten of its 116 posts discussed specific cases of fashion copycatting. The remaining 106 posts focus on a wide range of social justice issues including protests against anti-Black racism and state violence; transphobia; the racist associations of COVID-19 with Asians; the unequal access to COVID-19 testing across racial and class differences; celebrity obliviousness with regard to their quarantine privilege; the racist labor practices of brands like Anthropologie and *V Magazine*; fashion's co-optation of political movements; the problem of racist mascots and racist statues; and the mass closures of polling places in predominantly Black and Brown neighborhoods and regions.

Fittingly, a recent post in June 2020 is a multipart takedown of *Vogue* magazine. In a series of nine images, each titled "American Vogue's Most Problematic Moments," it recounts the magazine's various screw-ups from its many racist editorials to its elevation of a dictator's wife.[50] Diet Prada's willingness to call out what is arguably the most influential fashion magazine in the world, run by the industry's foremost gatekeeper, simultaneously illustrates the Instagram watchdog's outsider status and its outsized power. The post, tagged with the labels #annawintour, #whiteprivilege, and #blacklivesmatter, currently has 270,037 likes—more than four times the number of likes that a *Vogue* Instagram post received on the same day.

Why We Can't Have Nice Things

During an interview in 2018, Miuccia Prada stated, "Nobody actually cares about authenticity anymore. . . . No one talks about authenticity, with the exception of . . . a few extravagant intellectuals maybe. As a concept, it's not relevant anymore."[1] What strikes me about her words—besides her explicit dig at "a few extravagant intellectuals"—is that Prada is both right and wrong about the predominant attitude toward "authentic" fashion and fashion knockoffs.

Obviously, defining and policing the line between authentic and inauthentic fashion and, more often, legitimate and illegitimate copies is as important today as ever. We've seen this throughout this book. As I complete *Nice Things*, a number of brands, including Tory Burch, Missoni, Dolce & Gabbana, Alice + Olivia, and others, have just launched antipiracy campaigns on the Chinese-owned video-sharing site TikTok. The campaigns—part brand promotion and part public education—aren't being created "in-house" by a brand's marketing or legal team. The work of creating and maintaining them is being digitally outsourced (rather than broadly crowdsourced) to specific TikTok "influencers."

Brands are tapping some of the most popular social media users to promote their antipiracy messages. These "influencers" preemptively agree to make videos that "show how high quality and great the [original] product is," to affix the brand's hashtag to the video they've made, and to post it to their personal TikTok accounts where they've built large followings.[2] For this, they may get a nominal fee (per post or per new follower), some clothes or a handbag, and the cultural capital that comes with being associated with a luxury brand. These kinds of agreements represent both the professionalization of fashion consumer labor and the gigification of crowdsourced fashion intellectual property (IP) regulatory work (with all the risks of economic precarity and vulnerability that contingent employment entails).

The COVID-19 pandemic has also sparked renewed and racialized concerns about the authenticity of goods arriving to the United States. Donald Trump's trade war with China intensified the racial framing of antipiracy rhetoric and the efforts to halt the importation of knockoffs, particularly Chinese-produced fashions, at the border. As COVID-19 ripped through the United States, the anti-Asian politics of the trade war, the pandemic, and fake fashion came to a head in the development and application of Chinese-targeted trade policies. In Florida, Republican senator Rick Scott ordered US Customs and Border Protection agents at the Port of Miami to increase "screenings and inspections for [counterfeit] goods coming in from China," citing "the growing threat of the *Chinese coronavirus.*"[3] Never mind that "authentic" goods—particularly the fashion products that tend to be the focus of these screenings—are also made in China.[4]

The reality of global manufacturing aside, the mass media coverage of state agents seizing (racially contaminated) fashion knockoffs just before they cross Western national/market borders contributes to a myth about the ethical purity or authenticity of Western designs and markets (e.g., the idea that Western-made products are more ethically produced than Asian-made products). This myth rests on the construction and exclusion of unethical fashion others. Today, the myth of Western authenticity—often described as "our intellectual property" (see chapter 2)—is embedded in trade protectionist rhetoric and policies. The myth makes it possible to portray Western states and corporations as victims of globalization rather than its chief beneficiaries. In this upside-down narrative, globalization is seen as making Western innovator countries and citizens vulnerable to ethically foreign invaders when, in fact, globalization has been the primary means by which the West has converged on and benefited from the geo-political-economic vulnerability of Global South workers. The idea that (Western) authenticity needs protection serves to legitimize xenophobic beliefs that international trade agreements and IP rights governing bodies (like the US Customs and Border Protection agency) are mechanisms of self-defense rather than tools of racial-colonial economic domination.

That said, Miuccia Prada is also right that "nobody actually cares about authenticity anymore." After all, antipiracy campaigns wouldn't be necessary if there wasn't a demand for knockoffs, if consumers weren't actively seeking out and buying knockoffs—often on the same social media sites where they're naming and shaming fashion copycats. On Instagram, the number of accounts promoting and selling fashion knockoffs rose 171 percent between 2016 and 2019.[5] These accounts are estimated to have "cumulatively added more than 65 million posts to Instagram" and "average about 1.6 million Instagram Stories a month."[6] On TikTok, one of the most popular categories of "how-to" videos are the ones that focus on "how to find 'dupes,' or . . . items that look like Chanel, Gucci, Lululemon, Louis Vuitton and Cartier or other pricey designers—not to expose and shame the retailers but to buy from them. Other videos show how TikTok users actually make do-it-yourself designer dupes."[7] On Reddit, numerous subreddits or topic-based community forums are dedicated to all manner of information about fashion copies. One example is r/RepLadies, which has been described as "a community that revels in the granular buying process of finding, locating, and shipping fake goods."[8] The group, which leans toward the more expensive "supercopies" market, maintains a catalog of trusted and dodgy sellers and meticulously documents the quality of items they sell. R/RepLadies has 92,000 members.[9] Another subreddit is r/Repsneakers. As the name suggests, it focuses on replica luxury sneakers from brands like Balenciaga and Dior. Like r/RepLadies, the discussion is far ranging—where to find and buy replica sneakers, information on trusted sellers, exegeses about the quality of a particular pair of replica sneakers, and the ethical implications of replica fashions. This group has 242,000 members.[10]

Miuccia Prada's assessment is both right and wrong because contemporary fashion is caught in a contradictory moment. Social media has enabled fashion producers and consumers to be more ethically conscious and to express their fashion ethics in ways that weren't possible before. *At the same time*, the market for all kinds of fashion copies has only grown with social media. The contradiction is typical of popular culture, which is always constituted by a contradictory mix of social, cultural, economic, and ideological forces. Popular culture, in the language of cultural studies scholarship, is "a contested terrain" and people, especially in their capacity as consumers, are contradictory subjects. The contradiction, in and of itself then, is not revealing. A more instructive expression of this contradictory moment is the Western "real fake" trend in which North American and European designer and luxury brands, many of which have cried copycat, are now designing products that blatantly mimic knockoff aesthetics.

A "real fake" example in the luxury sector is the Louis Vuitton collection of bags designed in collaboration with artist Jeff Koons. The handbags and backpacks feature Koons's hand-painted reproductions of famous paintings such as Da Vinci's *Mona Lisa* and Van Gogh's *Wheat Field with Cypresses*, the name of the original artist in big gold letters, and a scattering of Louis Vuitton logos. Fans and critics alike compared them to Chinese or Chinatown knockoffs. Another example is the intentionally misspelled "Guccy" collection designed for Gucci by Trevor Andrew a.k.a. GucciGhost in 2016. Andrew attracted Gucci's notice because he was using the label's trademarked double-G logo as his tagger name or graffiti signature. Two years later, Gucci would collaborate with another artist whom, in the 1980s, it threatened to sue for IP infringement: Daniel Day a.k.a. Dapper Dan.[11] The 2018 collaboration came about after social media users called out Gucci for copying Dapper Dan's signature cut-and-mix aesthetic and specifically one of his jackets for its Cruise Collection. Gucci's partnership with Dapper Dan means that it now commercially and culturally profits from rather than competes with the popular designer. Finally, there's the Vetements Official Fake Collection produced exclusively for the South Korean market. The collection consists of the brand's most popular pieces "altered ever so slightly for the 'fake' look."[12]

"Real fakes" at the midmarket level exist too. One example is House of 950's "flawed T-shirts," which feature a shaky Nike swoosh symbol and an equally shaky sentiment ("Maybe I'll do it"—also embroidered badly). Another example is Diesel's misspelled "Deisel" line of hats, T-shirts, and sweatshirts. By misspelling its own name and by opening a pop-up "Deisel" store right off of Canal Street in Manhattan's Chinatown, the brand is giving a nod and a wink to the racist associations of knockoff fashions with Chinese people—while entirely missing the Chinese history of the branded fake.[13] According to Fan Yang, China may have invented the branded fake. The term "shanzhai," she argues, doesn't just describe fake products; it circulates in the market as a "'brand name' for the fake."[14] The very question of its origins underscores a central argument in this book—real and fake fashion aren't things but instead racialized sites of struggle over value, meaning, and power.

The Western real fake trend is an intentional and obvious contradiction in terms. As a concept, it's also contradictory—though in unintentional ways. The knockoff aesthetics they feature—misspelled words, shoddy stitching, and flashy logos—reference the racist and classist assumptions about what fashion knockoffs look like and where they come from in order to mock them. (Note that these "real fakes" look nothing like the meticulous supercopies made in Korea and China and gloss over the other kind of Western fakes that are swept under the rubrics of cultural appropriation or cultural inspiration.) Real fakes are at once objects of derision and desire. They signify low social status *and*, as luxury and designer products, they convey prestige. They're expressions of both bad taste and *ironically* bad taste. They take swipes at (budget) knockoff producers in an effort to beat them at their own game, but real fakes have also helped to destigmatize knockoffs and, in some ways, increase their appeal.

The contradictions recall for me the tradition of race and class tourism called "slumming," in which white middle- and upper-class people take pleasure in experiencing racial difference and poverty—what bell hooks called "eating the other"—as a temporary escape from their bourgeois lives.[15] Real fakes are means of wearing working-class identities while announcing one's social, cultural, and economic privileges. Although names like "official fakes" or "ironic fakes" suggest that the trend blurs racial and economic lines of taste, they actually sharpen them. They function overtly and/or implicitly as classist and racist jokes about working-class tastes that only middle-class and affluent white consumers can afford to enjoy, first, because of the prohibitively high cost of many of these objects and, second, because the costs of appearing to have bad taste and appearing to be poor are generally too high a price to pay for nonwhite consumers.

Although the "real fake" trend can offer only an ambivalent verdict on whether anyone really cares about authenticity anymore, it provides a much stronger case for arguing that the core principles and claims of the mainstream ethical fashion debate are not only *not* useful but also potentially misleading. Distinctions between authentic fashion and fashion knockoffs, legitimate copies and illegitimate ones, inspiration and imitation assume these categories name actual things with intrinsic qualities that can be defined and evaluated. But as I've been insisting throughout this book, these categories are better understood not as things but as expressions of asymmetrical power relations.

Real fake products are responses to economic not ethical challenges. They're market-competitive moves that draw on racial and class stereotypes to assert Western brand superiority at a time when Asian design and retail industries are becoming more globally competitive. Mainstream fashion ethical discourses, norms, and frameworks, whether they're produced by trained professionals or are crowdsourced or digitally outsourced to social media users, are about power. More often than not, they function to maintain social and market hierarchies through the unequal distribution of the right to copy and, with it, the unequal distribution of the privileges and profit that flow from this informal right. And today, social media users are the often-unwitting if well-intentioned agents of global fashion's asymmetrical power structure.

Until we grapple with fashion's entrenched power imbalances, including the authority to define and profit from what counts as ethical and unethical fashion practices, nice things like genuinely ethical fashion will only ever be fake.

INTRODUCTION. "SHARE THIS WITH YOUR FRIENDS"

1 Granted Sweater Company (@grantedsweatercompany), Instagram post, January 6, 2015, https://www.instagram.com/p/xhqXtKIoAV/.

2 Granted Sweater Company, Facebook post, January 6, 2015, https://www .facebook.com/grantedsweaters/photos/pb.28973649640.-2207520000 .1465225497./10152939439194641/?type=3&theater.

3 These quotes are from comments on the Facebook post.

4 This quote is from a comment on the Facebook post.

5 I use "fashion consumers" and "social media users" as shorthand terms that name broad, overlapping, and heterogeneous groups of people whose relationships to the fashion industry may be formal or informal, close or distant.

6 Radin, "How a Copyright Loophole Gave Birth."

7 Some examples of digital labor include cultural content production (Lazzarato, "Immaterial Labor"), online community managing (Nakamura, "The Unwanted Labour of Social Media"; Jarrett, *Feminism, Labour, and Digital Media*), content moderation (Chen, "The Laborers Who Keep Dick Pics"), data sanitation (Irani, "Justice for 'Data Janitors'"), social media influencing (Marwick and boyd, "To See and Be Seen"; Duffy, *[Not] Getting Paid to Do What You Love*), and fashion blogging (Pham, *Asians Wear Clothes on the Internet*).

8 Coombe, "Culture"; Pang, *Cultural Control and Globalization in Asia.*

9 Coombe, "Culture," 262.

10 Coombe, "Culture," 263.

11 Schultz, "Copynorms," 201.

12 Greene, "'Copynorms.'"

13 In the United States, more than eighty bills to extend the Copyright Act to include fashion design have been proposed, introduced, and reintroduced in Congress since 1914 (Colman, "The History and Principles of American Copyright Protection"). None have passed. The most recent ones were a Bill to Provide Protection for Fashion Design, introduced by Representative Robert Goodlatte in 2006. The bill sought to include fashion design as a protected category under the Vessel Hull Design Protection Act of the Digital Millennium Copyright Act. In 2007, Representative William Delahunt proposed a similar bill called the Design Piracy Prohibition Act (DPPA). In 2009, Delahunt reintroduced a revised version of the DPPA. In 2010, Senator Charles Schumer

introduced the Innovative Design Protection and Piracy Prevention Act (IDPPPA or ID3PA), then revised it in 2012 to require that a written notice be given before beginning legal action. Despite more than a century of industry lobbying and corporate and media activism, fashion design is not copyrightable in either the United States or Canada. Specific and purely decorative features like nongeneric fabric prints, logos, brooches, and belt buckles—things that are separable, if only conceptually, from the utilitarian function of the fashion product—are protectable under US and Canadian copyright, trademark, trade dress, and design patent laws.

14　Blakley, "Lessons from Fashion's Free Culture."

15　Quoted in Pouillard, "Design Piracy," 341.

16　It's worth noting that while there are legal distinctions between an actual counterfeit, an item that infringes on a trademark, and a "knockoff," parsing them doesn't occupy a significant place in the public discourse. For that reason, they don't occupy a significant place in this book. What I'm interested in is the conflation of these terms, how they operate in the public discourse not as legal terms but as cultural idioms and economic forces of racialized entitlement, power, and exclusion.

17　Quoted in Pike, "The Copycat Economy."

18　Quoted in Paul, "Is Social Media the New Court of Law?"

19　Raymond Williams, *Culture and Materialism*, 50.

20　Despite the exhibition's expressed Chinese theme, the featured pieces drew on a mix of Chinese, Japanese, and European chinoiserie. For more on the exhibition, see my essay *"China Through the Looking Glass."*

21　Nicolas Ghesquière (see the discussion in this introduction) became a prominent signatory to an amicus brief in support of Apple's lawsuit against Samsung because of its implications for fashion designers.

22　Larocca, "Fashion Police."

23　Frankel, "Ready to Wear."

24　Larocca, "Fashion Police."

25　See Spindler, "A Ruling by French Court," and Boyle, "Christian Louboutin Sues Yves Saint Laurent."

26　Ewick and Silbey, *The Common Place of Law*, 20.

27　Ewick and Silbey, *The Common Place of Law*, 22.

28　Binkley, "From the Runway to Your Laptop."

29　Copping, "Style Bloggers Take Centre Stage."

30　I write about the politicization of fashion after September 11 in "The Right to Fashion in the Age of Terrorism."

31　Bush, "A Nation Challenged," B4.

32　Halston's JCPenney line predates Mizrahi's Target line by two decades, but it was much less successful. The collaboration also damaged Halston's professional ties and reputation: "Not wanting a secondary association with the masses, Bergdorf Goodman dropped him . . . and the name Halston itself became a joke, even providing what is now depressing fodder for *Saturday Night Live*" (Odell, "From the Disco to JCPenney").

33 Murphy, "Mass Couture."

34 Brooks, "Stuff and Nonsense," A25.

35 Quoted in Stephenson and Strugatz, "Social Media."

36 Both campaigns launched in 2011.

37 In "The High Cost of High Fashion," I wrote about the prevalence and problems of these race- and class-based ethical fashion truisms. Examples of the budget fashion / fake fashion conflation can be found in almost any discussion about "fast fashion" or fashion copies. Three cases in point are Lieber, "Why the $600 Billion Counterfeit Industry Is Still Horrible for Fashion"; *Business of Fashion*, "What Are the Consequences of Copycats?"; and Coscarelli, "12 Fashion Knockoffs."

38 Terranova, "Free Labor."

39 See Elizabeth Verklan's article "Doing What You Love in the Age of Mass Debt" for an important discussion of the exploitative nature of fashion internships.

40 See Omi and Winant, *Racial Formation in the United States*.

41 Dean, *Democracy and Other Neoliberal Fantasies*, 26, 32, 43.

42 Dean, *Democracy and Other Neoliberal Fantasies*, 24.

43 Dean, *Democracy and Other Neoliberal Fantasies*, 27.

44 Dean, *Democracy and Other Neoliberal Fantasies*, 21.

I. REGULATING FASHION IP, REGULATING DIFFERENCE

1 Since 1931, more than sixty bills have been introduced and reintroduced to Congress; each of them, including the most recent bill, named the Innovative Design Protection Act of 2012, failed to pass. (For more, see note 30 in Schmidt, "Designer Law.")

2 For discussions of this point, see Nystrom, *Economics of Fashion*, and Meiklejohn, "Dresses."

3 Kal Raustiala and Christopher Sprigman's analysis of the piracy paradox is detailed and comprehensive. They developed this thesis in numerous mainstream and scholarly articles, including "The Piracy Paradox" and "The Piracy Paradox Revisited" (a rebuttal to C. Scott Hemphill and Jeannie Suk's criticism of their main thesis), as well as in their book, *The Knockoff Economy*. Other scholars like David Bollier and Laurie Racine (in "Ready to Share"), Jennifer Jenkins (quoted in E. Klein, "Copycats vs. Copyrights"), and Renee Richardson Gosline (in "The Real Value of Fakes") have argued similar points.

4 Quoted in Marcketti and Parsons, "Design Piracy and Self-Regulation," 217.

5 The standard markup percentage for retail fashion is between 55 and 62 percent. My estimate for the 2021 value is roughly based on a 50 percent markup. I used the officialdata.org inflation calculator to determine what in 2021 would be the equivalent purchasing power of $22.50 in 1932.

6   Hemphill and Suk, "The Fashion Originators' Guild of America," 162–63.

7   Jablow, interview.

8   Jablow, interview.

9   Jablow, interview.

10 *Women's Wear Daily*, "Formal Turbans and Square Crowns," 45.

11 See Hemphill and Suk, "The Fashion Originators' Guild of America," 162–63. See also *Women's Wear Daily*, "Guild Not to Copy Models of Retailers."

12 From Justice Black's ruling opinion in *Fashion Originators' Guild of America v. FTC*, 312 US 457 (1941).

13 Hemphill and Suk, "The Fashion Originators' Guild of America," 163.

14 Hemphill and Suk, "The Fashion Originators' Guild of America," 163.

15 Perhaps to preserve its access to exclusive fashion brands and a major source of advertising revenue, the fashion media has tended to act more like corporate sponsors than industry watchdogs. FOGA's ethical fashion campaign, like corporate-led campaigns today, represents an alliance between these two Big Fashion entities. For example, *Vogue* and *Women's Wear Daily* legitimized FOGA's campaign with copious media coverage and ad space and practically no coverage of grassroots campaigns like the "Don't Buy" movement. Searching the *Vogue* and *Women's Wear Daily* archives, I found only one mention of the Black community-led "Don't Buy" movement: a two-inch article published in 1960 that reported on the arrest of six "Don't Buy" activists in New Orleans rather than their political objectives. See Marcketti, "Design Piracy in the United States"; Marcketti and Parsons, "Design Piracy and Self-Regulation"; and *Women's Wear Daily*, "6 Pickets Arrested in New Orleans."

    The Rentner quotation is from Marcketti and Parsons, "Design Piracy and Self-Regulation," 220.

16 *New York Times*, "Hits Garment Practices."

17 Soyer, "The Rise and Fall of the Garment Industry in New York City," 3.

18 Rantisi, "The Ascendance of New York Fashion."

19 Wolcott, "Adolf Hitler: Grand Couturier," 327.

20 Rantisi, "The Ascendance of New York Fashion," 92.

21 Marcketti and Parsons, "Design Piracy and Self-Regulation," 225.

22 Marcketti, "Design Piracy in the United States," 99.

23 Marcketti and Parsons, "Design Piracy and Self-Regulation," 217.

24 *Women's Wear Daily*, "Protecting Originality."

25 *Vogue*, "Piracy on the High Fashions," 28.

26 See, for example, Cornelius, "American Designer Movement," and Robinson, "America Dresses Herself."

27 Gino, Norton, and Ariely, "The Counterfeit Self"; Herbert, "We're Only Human," 67.

28 Herbert, "We're Only Human," 66; Gino, Norton, and Ariely, "The Counterfeit Self."

29 Mirghani, "The War on Piracy," 120.

30 *Women's Wear Daily*, "$1.37 to $6.75 Dress Concerns."

31 Lawrence B. Glickman provides a fascinating account of this early period of nineteenth-century consumer activism in his essay "'Buy for the Sake of the Slave.'" For culture jamming, see Coombe and Herman, "Culture Wars on the Internet," and Coombe and Herman, "Trademarks, Property, and Propriety."

32 Higgins, "Use Your Buying Power for Justice," 44.

33 There's no evidence that the League of Women Shoppers ever drew connections between the treatment of Chinese people by Japanese imperialists and the racist treatment of Chinese people in the United States. An ignored irony is that while the LWS was urging women to boycott Japanese silk stockings to "keep the figurative blood and bones of Chinese babies from around their legs," its activities emerged against the backdrop of the Asian exclusion era (quoted in Glickman, "'Make Lisle the Style,'" 591–92). Decades of intensifying anti-Asian sentiment and policies culminated with a series of federal immigration acts excluding, first, Chinese women then eventually all people from the so-called Asiatic Barred Zone. Poignantly, the first of these acts, the 1875 Page Act, sought to prevent the births of Chinese American babies by barring Chinese women from entry to the United States.

34 Higgins, "Use Your Buying Power for Justice," 51, 45.

35 Sundstrom, "Last Hired, First Fired?"

36 *Fashion Originators' Guild of America v. FTC*, 312 US 457 (1941).

37 Clifford, "Economic Indicator." See also Committee on International Relations, "Intellectual Property Crimes."

38 The International Anti-counterfeiting Coalition estimate is from Patry, *Moral Panics and the Copyright Wars*, 33. The Conyers estimate is from Patry, *Moral Panics and the Copyright Wars*, 34.

39 See for example, Bukszpan, "Counterfeiting"; Lieber, "Why the $600 Billion Counterfeit Industry Is Still Horrible for Fashion"; Shenkar, *The Chinese Century*, 94; D. Thomas, *Deluxe*, 274; and Tirrell, "Fake Louis Vuitton Bags." This is by no means an exhaustive list, but it indicates the range of sources that perpetuate this fake statistic.

40 For sources that debunk the figures, see Masnick, "Hey NY Times"; Salmon, "All Counterfeiting Statistics Are Bullshit"; Salmon, "CNBC Embarrasses Itself on Counterfeiting"; Salmon, "Counterfeiting"; and Sanchez, "750,000 Lost Jobs?"

41 US Government Accountability Office, "Intellectual Property, Reporting to the Ranking Member" 17, 28.

42 US Government Accountability Office, "Intellectual Property, Observations on Efforts," 26.

43 US Government Accountability Office, "Intellectual Property, Observations on Efforts," 27.

44 Quoted in Patry, *Moral Panics and the Copyright Wars*, 33.

45 US Copyright Office, "Statement of the United States Copyright Office."

46 US Government Publishing Office, "Hearing before the Subcommittee on Intellectual Property, Competition, and the Internet," 83.

47 Patry, *Moral Panics and the Copyright Wars*, 35.

48 Lieber, "Fashion Brands Steal Design Ideas All the Time."

49 Fashion trials by social media are routinely viewed positively as vigilantism. See Radin, "How a Copyright Loophole Gave Birth"; Dorking, "Why Social Media Shaming Is Calling Out Fashion Copycats"; and Yi, "How Social Media Shaming Controls Fashion Copycats."

50 Scholars working at the intersection of critical race, indigeneity, and property studies are too many to name, but my research is indebted especially to the work of Jane E. Anderson (*Law, Knowledge, Culture*); Keith Aoki ("Foreignness and Asian American Identities"; "[Intellectual] Property and Sovereignty"; "Neocolonialism, Anticommons Property, and Biopiracy"), Derrick Bell (*Faces at the Bottom of the Well*), Boatema Boateng (*The Copyright Thing Doesn't Work Here*), Anupam Chander and Madhavi Sunder ("The Romance of the Public Domain"), Rosemary J. Coombe (*The Cultural Life of Intellectual Properties*), Ruth Gana ("The Myth of Development, the Progress of Rights"), Cheryl L. Harris ("Whiteness as Property"), Adrian Johns (*Piracy*), George Lipsitz (*The Possessive Investment in Whiteness*), Chidi Oguamanam (*International Law and Indigenous Knowledge*), Kavita Philip ("What Is a Technological Author?"), Trevor Reed ("Who Owns Our Ancestors' Voices?"), Vandana Shiva (*Biopiracy*), Rebecca Tsosie ("Who Controls Native Cultural Heritage?"), and Anjali Vats and Deidre A. Keller ("Critical Race IP"; Vats, *The Color of Creatorship*).

51 Harris, "Whiteness as Property," 1734.

52 Harris, "Whiteness as Property," 1731.

53 Harris, "Whiteness as Property," 1731.

54 *Johnson v. M'Intosh*, 21 US 543, 573 (1823).

55 Vats, "(Dis)Owning Bikram," 9.

56 Vats, "(Dis)Owning Bikram," 9.

57 Fredriksson, "Piracy, Globalisation, and the Colonisation of the Commons."

58 Fredriksson, "Piracy, Globalisation, and the Colonisation of the Commons," 3.

59 Chander and Sunder, "The Romance of the Public Domain," 1335.

60 Metcalfe, "Misappropriation and the Case of the Yellow Crotch."

61 Larsson, "Inspiration or Plagiarism?"

62 See *Fashion Law*, "Isabel Marant Wins Case over 'Stolen' Tribal Design."

63 *Antik Batik SASU v. I.M. Production SAS*, No. 15/03456 (2015). SASU and SAS are acronyms for the legal designations of small business entities. They're primarily used to identify the company's tax bracket. SASU stands for Société par Actions Simplifiées Unipersonnelle and SAS stands for Société par Actions Simplifiées.

64 *Antik Batik SASU v. I.M. Production SAS*, No. 15/03456 (2015). (All translations of the court transcripts are mine.)

65 The court transcripts mention two letters written by Mexican citizens who arranged and guided Marant's trip to Santa Maria Tlahuitoltepec, where the inspiration for her blouses was born. The transcript and the Tlahuitoltepec people's public statements therein stated that despite their requests, "extended in multiple ways, there has been no contact from Isabel Marant whatsoever." (See *Fashion Law*, "Isabel Marant Wins Case over 'Stolen' Tribal Design.")

The Regino Montes quotation is from *Yucatan Times*, "Indigenous Oaxacans Challenge French Label."

66 *Antik Batik SASU v. I.M. Production SAS*, No. 15/03456 (2015).

67 Faris, "Can a Tribe Sue for Copyright?"

68 *Fashion Law*, "Isabel Marant Wins Case over 'Stolen' Tribal Design"; Szmydke, "Isabel Marant Cleared of Plagiarism Allegations."

69 Cited in *Fashion Law*, "Isabel Marant Wins Case over 'Stolen' Tribal Design."

70 Varagur, "Mexico Prevents Indigenous Designs from Being Culturally Appropriated—Again."

71 See Contreras, "Isabel Marant and Antik Batik."

72 See Gana, "The Myth of Development, the Progress of Rights"; Shiva, *Biopiracy*; and Aoki, "Neocolonialism, Anticommons Property, and Biopiracy."

73 Pang, *Creativity and Its Discontents*, 9.

74 Pang, *Creativity and Its Discontents*, 16.

75 Shiva, *Biopiracy*, 9–10.

76 The 2010 revenue figure is from Pasquarelli, "40 Under 40: Shirley Cook, 32"; the 2015 figure is from Silver, "Proenza Schouler Gets a Major Push from a Minority Investment."

77 Trebay, "An Uneasy Cultural Exchange," E1.

78 Trebay, "An Uneasy Cultural Exchange," E1.

2. THE ASIAN FASHION COPYCAT

1 The term *shanzhai* literally refers to a mountain stronghold of Robin Hood–like bandits but is now understood as the name for Chinese (and sometimes Korean) copycat products and cultural practices.

2 Some representative works are Pang, *Creativity and Its Discontents*; Yang, *Faked in China*; and Liao, *Fashioning China*.

3 Pang, *Creativity and Its Discontents*, 189, 192.

4 Lessig, *Free Culture*, ix.

5 Philip, "What Is a Technological Author?," 212.

6 Kacynski, "Carly Fiorina."

7 For Warren, see *Reuters*, "United States Waking Up to Chinese Abuses." For Bannon, see J. Green, "Bannon's Back and Targeting China."

8 See Magni and Atsmon, "China's Luxury Consumers Grow Up." Here's a brief list of articles that use the language of "maturity" to discuss Asian fashion

tastes: Dodd, "China Chic, Not China Cheap"; Davey-Attlee, "Why China Is Sitting on Fashion's Front Row"; Menkes, "The Asian Wave"; Jung-a, "Luxury Brands Battle to Stay in Fashion in South Korea"; and Master, "Bottom Line."

9 China has been the prime, but not exclusive, target of these civilizing efforts. Meanwhile, Japan for now has been exempt from fashion's civilizing mission.

10 Quoted in Karabell, "Too Much Demand, Too Little Space."

11 Quoted in Branigan, "China's Taste for High-End Fashion."

12 Emphasis added. Hall, "Cracks Appear in China's Fashion Magazine Landscape."

13 Hall, "Cracks Appear in China's Fashion Magazine Landscape."

14 Quoted in Bradsher, "Chinese Apparel Makers Increasingly Seek the Creative Work."

15 Quoted in Bradsher, "Chinese Apparel Makers Increasingly Seek the Creative Work."

16 See, for example, Hall, "A Turning Point," and Yin, "Alibaba Vows to Carry On Fake Goods Crackdown."

17 Newman, *White Women's Rights*, 8.

18 Newman, *White Women's Rights*, 8–9.

19 Rapp, "Two Chinese Copycat Fashion Brands."

20 Sun, "The Wild, Wild East."

21 Sherman, "Are Fakes Back in Fashion?"

22 *Fashion Law*, "Are Your 'Made in China' Luxury Goods Just as Luxurious?"

23 Martha Stewart, Twitter post, April 24, 2014, 3:36 p.m., https://twitter.com /marthastewart/status/459415578013605888.

24 See Kitroeff and Kim, "Behind a $13 Shirt"; Kitroeff, "Factories That Made Clothes for Forever 21"; and Hines, "Forever 21 under Investigation."

25 *Economist*, "Long-Term Chinese Immigrants in Italy."

26 Quoted in Spence, *The Chan's Great Continent*, 40.

27 Kim, "Asian Americans and American Popular Culture," 106.

28 Quoted in Chang, *The Chinese in America*, 130.

29 See Aoki, "Foreign-ness and Asian American Identities," 24.

30 London, *Revolution and Other Essays*, 311.

31 London, *Revolution and Other Essays*, 310.

32 Colleen Lye provides a discussion of the various myths about Japanese Americans that emerged in the 1940s in her book *America's Asia: Racial Form and American Literature, 1893–1945*.

33 Quoted in Johns, *Piracy*, 449.

34 Mentioned in Perzanowski and Schultz, *The End of Ownership*, 126.

35 Cited in Johns, *Piracy*, 454.

36 Drucker, "Japan's Choices."

37 Aoki, "Foreign-ness and Asian American Identities," 43.

38 Morley and Robins, *Spaces of Identity*, 172.

39 See Petersen, "Success Story, Japanese American Style"; *Newsweek*, "Success Story"; *US News and World Report*, "Success Story"; and *Los Angeles Times*, "Japanese in U.S. Outdo Horatio Alger."

40 Lye, *America's Asia*, 5.

41 Wohlsen, "Alibaba Now Worth More Than Facebook, Amazon, and IBM."

42 Emarketer.com, "Ecommerce Continues Strong Gains."

43 China's e-commerce boom is the result of several major factors: (1) its widespread use of artificial intelligence and big data analytics across the retail chain "from design to shelf," including in the design of high-performance textiles, production scheduling, trend forecasting, and delivery systems; (2) its early adoption and development of mobile e-commerce platforms and financial services; and (3) state-driven initiatives and investments committed to giving China a stronger foothold in higher-value manufacturing and retail activities. See *Singapore Business Review*, "Asia E-commerce Market."

44 L. Thomas, "Store Closures Rocked Retail in 2017."

45 *Business of Fashion* and McKinsey and Company, "The State of Fashion: 2018," 11.

46 Barua, "Asia's Retail Spending Boom."

47 Barua, "Asia's Retail Spending Boom."

48 Aoki, "The Yellow Pacific."

49 Lacy, "Why 2018 Was the 'Year of Ecommerce' in Southeast Asia."

50 Yang, *Faked in China*, 68–69.

51 See chapter 2 in Yang's book *Faked in China*.

52 Clover, "Alibaba's Jack Ma Says Fakes Are Better Than Originals."

53 Quoted in Dou, "Jack Ma Says Fakes 'Better Quality.'"

54 See, for example, S. Lazzaro, "All Signs Point to Scam"; Forster, "Disappointed Customers"; Coscarelli, "Here's What Happened"; and Ferrier, "This Is What Happens When You Order."

55 A *New York Times* profile of Allen Schwartz in the Home and Garden section portrays him as a charming nonconformist with an impeccable sense of interior design. See Wadler, "Remaking the Scene," D1.

56 Wilson, "Before Models Can Turn Around, Knockoffs Fly," A1.

57 Wilson, "Before Models Can Turn Around, Knockoffs Fly," A1.

58 US Government Publishing Office, "Innovative Design Protection and Piracy Prevention Act."

59 von Furstenberg, "Fashion Deserves Copyright Protection."

60 Cline, *Overdressed*, 109.

61 Research on search-engine bias has been ongoing since at least the days of Web 1.0. See, for example, Gonzalez and Rodriguez, "Filipinas.com"; Arreola, "Latinas"; Noble, "Missed Connections"; Noble, *Algorithms of Oppression*; Gillespie, "The Relevance of Algorithms"; and Benjamin, *Race after Technology*.

62 Gillespie, "The Relevance of Algorithms," 172.

63 Chow-White, "The Informationalization of Race," 1169.

64 Harris, "Whiteness as Property," 1721.

65 Your Source for All Things Ghetto, Twitter post, June 24, 2010, 11:33 p.m., https://twitter.com/LovevsMoney/status/16984790713.

66 Midler, *Poorly Made in China*, 116.

67 Emphasis added. Ellis, "Report Sees China Counterfeiting Worsen," 2.

68 Quoted in Cook, "Why South Korea Is the Home of Counterfeit Culture."

69 See Khagi, "Who's Afraid of Forever 21?"; Yi, "How Social Media Shaming Controls Fashion Copycats"; Colon, "This Design from Forever 21"; and Kaplan, "How Artists Are Fighting Back."

3. HOW THAI SOCIAL MEDIA USERS MADE BALENCIAGA PAY FOR COPYING THE SAMPENG BAG

1 As I've explained elsewhere, the racial, class, and geographic hierarchies embedded in the interpretative frameworks of cultural appropriation and cultural appreciation led to the wrong conclusions about the bag's provenance. These large, plastic, plaid-printed carryalls are popular not only in US Chinatowns but also in various parts of Asia and Africa. The bags' distinctive plaid patterns, though, are copies of textile prints that were historically reserved for Indonesia's upper class. Therefore, Céline, Stella McCartney, and Louis Vuitton knocked off knockoffs. See Pham, "Fashion's Cultural Appropriation Debate."

2 See, for example, More Milk (@moremilksut), Instagram post, March 7, 2016, https://www.instagram.com/p/BCrK66xl1I1/.

3 Edwards, "This Designer Bag."

4 Sowray, "Balenciaga's Striped Bags."

5 Graafland, "How Balenciaga's £975 Thai Market Stall–Inspired Bag"; Sowray, "Balenciaga's Striped Bags"; Porter, "You Can Now Buy Balenciaga's 'Laundry Bags' for over $2,000."

6 See, for example, *Bangkok Post*, "'Rainbow Tote' Latest Fashion Statement," and Hernitaningtyas, "This Is Why Balenciaga's Latest Tote Bags Are Trending."

7 *Malay Mail*, "Why Thais Are Having a Good Chuckle."

8 boyd, "Social Network Sites as Networked Publics," 48.

9 The United States didn't recognize hashtags as trademarkable until 2013, three years after some European countries.

10 McDowell, "Protecting Fashion Hashtags with Trademarks."

11 Marshall, "Companies Increasingly Trademark Hashtags."

12 Sherwin, "#HaveWeReallyThoughtThisThrough?"

13 Sherwin, "#HaveWeReallyThoughtThisThrough?," 478.

14 Sowray, "Balenciaga's Striped Bags."

15 When a hashtag spikes in use or "trends," trending algorithms push the hashtag into greater public visibility for search engine result lists, lists of trending tropics, and social media pages.

16 Dery, "The Merry Pranksters."

17 Dery, "Culture Jamming."

18 Lasn, *Culture Jam*, 103.

19 "Guerilla semiotics" is from Dery, "The Merry Pranksters"; "semiotic Robin Hoodism" is from N. Klein, *No Logo*; "rhetorical jujitsu" is from Harold, "Pranking Rhetoric"; and for an array of parody, gripe, and "suck" websites, see Coombe and Herman, "Culture Wars on the Internet," and Coombe and Herman, "Trademarks, Property, and Propriety."

20 See Coombe and Herman, "Culture Wars on the Internet," and Coombe and Herman, "Trademarks, Property, and Propriety."

21 Coombe and Herman, "Culture Wars on the Internet," 939.

22 Fernquest, "Fashion."

23 Wise Man, Facebook post, March 6, 2016, https://www.facebook.com /nukprach/photos/a.614641881891931/1033661109990004/?type=3&theater.

24 Many thanks to Wantana "Tik" Pokun for her help in translating parts of the Thai/Balenciaga meme.

25 These are some of the comments users left on the Wise Man Facebook post.

26 Eric Tobua (@erictobua), Instagram post, March 8, 2016, https://www .instagram.com/p/BCrjbnXh8Hw/.

27 A. Thomas, "Balenciaga Casts No Models of Color."

28 p.m.orm (@p.m.orm), Instagram post, March 9, 2016, https://www.instagram .com/p/BCuySmQHFqG/.

29 I discuss the spatiotemporal aesthetics of fashion blogger poses in detail in my book *Asians Wear Clothes on the Internet*.

30 I discuss this incident in greater detail in chapter 4.

31 Trebay, "At Marc Jacobs."

32 Isaac-Goizé, "They Only Skimped on the Fabric."

33 Metcalfe, "Misappropriation and the Case of the Yellow Crotch."

34 Fernquest, "Fashion."

35 This is a comment responding to Wise Man's Facebook post (cited earlier in this chapter's notes).

36 *Asia News Network*, "Thai Handbags Not Breaking Intellectual Property Laws."

37 *Asia News Network*, "Thai Handbags Not Breaking Intellectual Property Laws."

38 Foucault, *Abnormal*, 19.

39 Abbas, "Faking Globalization"; Boateng, *The Copyright Thing Doesn't Work Here*; Luvaas, "Designer Vandalism"; Luvaas, "Material Interventions"; Nakassis, "Brands and Their Surfeits"; Nakassis, "The Quality of a Copy"; K. Thomas, *Regulating Style*; and Vann, "The Limits of Authenticity."

40 Nakassis, "The Quality of a Copy," 158.

41 K. Thomas, *Regulating Style*, 109.

42 K. Thomas, *Regulating Style*, 109.

43 Vann, "The Limits of Authenticity," 290.

44 K. Thomas, *Regulating Style*, 93.

45 Luvaas, "Material Interventions," 137.

4. "PPL KNOCKING EACH OTHER OFF LOL"

1 Quoted in Sherman, "Diet Prada Unmasked."

2 Quoted in Sherman, "Diet Prada Unmasked."

3 Liu's menswear label is called You As.

4 Lanigan, "The Duo behind Diet Prada."

5 Farley, "How the Diet Prada Cofounders."

6 See Gerrie, "The Diet Prada Effect," and Lydia, "The Diet Prada Effect."

7 Estee Laundry (@esteelaundry), Instagram post, December 28, 2018, https://www.instagram.com/p/Br6zY6CHTm4/.

8 See Ritschel, "Stefano Gabbana," and Zane, "This Dolce & Gabbana T-shirt."

9 Counterfeit Culture, 2013.

10 The comparison example for the pumps and the instant ramen is from Diet Prada (@diet_prada)'s Instagram post on December 17, 2019, https://www.instagram.com/p/B6MVKL1HtEI/.

11 Katz, "Diet Prada Elevates Dolce & Gabbana Feud."

12 My understanding of this term comes from Adrienne Keene's important blog by the same name. Keene (a citizen of the Cherokee Nation) created *Native Appropriations*, a blog that focuses on the appropriation of not only Native fashions but also Native aesthetics, names, religions, and stories, in 2010 while attending graduate school. Today, Keene is a professor at Brown University and cohosts a popular podcast with Matika Wilbur (from the Swinomish and Tulalip peoples of coastal Washington State) called *All My Relations*.

13 Lipsky-Karasz, "Karl Lagerfeld Was Never Satisfied."

14 See, for example, Diet Prada's December 14, 2018, post (https://www.instagram.com/p/BrYU8M6l6Eq/) calling out its namesake and its January 19, 2018, post (https://www.instagram.com/p/BeKIh1vlfff/) calling out Gvasalia, a self-professed Diet Prada fan.

15 N. Klein, *No Logo*, 351.

16 For more on this, see the discussion about Nicolas Ghesquière and Kaisik Wong in the introduction and chapter 1.

17 Simpson, "Consent's Revenge," 328.

18 Simpson, "Consent's Revenge," 328.

19 Simpson, "Consent's Revenge," 328.

20 Simpson, "Consent's Revenge," 329.

21 Simpson, "Consent's Revenge," 329.

22 Liu and Schuyler typically use the collective "we" in their Diet Prada posts but in a small handful of posts that have to do with anti-Asian racism, Liu

addresses Diet Prada readers as an individual. It was in one of these more personal posts that we learn about his mom's work history in the garment industry. See Diet Prada (@diet_prada), Instagram post, November 22, 2018, https://www.instagram.com/p/BqgYeYHFT9i/.

23 Diet Prada (@diet_prada), Instagram post, May 15, 2018, https://www .instagram.com/p/BizhtM7gwI5/.

24 The Diet Prada (@diet_prada) Instagram post discussed here appeared on May 15, 2018 (the link is provided in note 23).

Target's corporate hypocrisy in relation to the queer community is well established. For years, it has partnered with queer fashion designers, including Isaac Mizrahi, Phillip Lim, and the Proenza Schouler founders, while also using corporate funds to support antigay organizations and right-wing politicians with antigay voting records. It was not until 2011 as part of a deal with Lady Gaga for the exclusive rights to sell a special edition of the single "Born This Way" that the corporation promised to "'make amends' and donate to gay rights groups." According to Pink News, Target "committed $500,000 to LGBT community projects" ("Target Agrees to Fund Gay Groups"). That number is approximately 0.3 percent of the $156 million Target donates annually to "community efforts" and 0.007 percent of the nearly $70 billion generated in the same year.

25 Target, "Target Corporation Annual Report: 2018," 3.

26 D'Eon mentions on his own Instagram account that he confirmed Lipchik's racial identity: "I've talked to him and he's not a Latinx person—and he was very supportive of my position." Felix d'Eon (@felixdeon), Instagram post, May 21, 2018, https://www.instagram.com/p/BjDPzpeArBG/.

27 Bromwich, "We're All Drinking Diet Prada Now."

28 Diet Prada (@diet_prada), Instagram post, February 11, 2019, https://www .instagram.com/p/BtvuGgYlrNi/.

29 The Diet Prada (@diet_prada) Instagram post discussed here appeared on May 15, 2018 (the link is provided in note 23).

30 See, for example, Taylor, "Target Quietly Removes a T-shirt."

31 Farley, "How the Diet Prada Cofounders."

32 Diet Prada (@diet_prada), Instagram post, October 23, 2017, https://www .instagram.com/p/Bana_fRFEuV/.

33 Brannigan, "Condé Nast Bans Terry Richardson."

34 See Mau, "Valentino Is the Latest Brand," and Friedman and Paton, "A Scapegoat for the Fashion Industry?"

35 Dowd, "The Vampire Is Vegan."

36 Arnett, "Valentino Is Luxury Fashion's Fastest-Growing Company."

37 Lasn, *Culture Jam*, 165–84.

38 The relevant Diet Prada Instagram posts appeared on July 22, 2019 (https:// www.instagram.com/p/BoOVdQHnfBu/?hl=en), July 23, 2019 (https://www .instagram.com/p/BoRaP2pHxzK/?hl=en), and November 24, 2019 (https://

www.instagram.com/p/B5QbCdPHwdT/). The Testino and Weber revelations shed important light on photographers' abuse of male models.

39 Diet Prada (@diet_prada), Instagram post, November 20, 2018 (https://www .instagram.com/p/BqbTkY_FB7X/).

40 The extended caption begins by mentioning Dolce & Gabbana's history of Orientalist appropriation ("chopsticks as hair ornaments, take-out boxes as purses, or even kimonos misappropriated as Chinese costume"). It goes on to suggest a labor boycott of the Shanghai show ("wouldn't let them walk the show if we were their agents lol") and that China bar the designers from entering the country by denying their visa applications ("curious what the Chinese government will think of their country being called shit basically . . . especially considering how strict they are on who to allow to enter the country on work visas based on a thorough social media background checks"). See Diet Prada (@diet_prada), Instagram post, November 20, 2018 (see the link in note 39).

41 *Dazed Digital*, "I Watched D&G's China Show."

42 *Dazed Digital*, "I Watched D&G's China Show."

43 Robert Williams, "Dolce & Gabbana Is Still Paying."

44 Robert Williams, "Dolce & Gabbana Is Still Paying."

45 This comes from the headline of the online version of Vanessa Friedman's article "The Resurrection of Dolce & Gabbana." The print version is titled "Fashion Brands Learn How to Survive a Storm."

46 Diet Prada (@diet_prada), Instagram post, June 13, 2019, https://www .instagram.com/p/Byp3ILaHmFr/.

47 NBC News, "Dolce & Gabbana Fiasco."

48 Barry, "Dolce & Gabbana Seeks over $600M Damages."

49 Diet Prada (@diet_prada), Instagram post, March 4, 2021, https://www .instagram.com/p/CMATJ4lH5k-/.

50 Diet Prada (@diet_prada), Instagram post, June 15, 2020, https://www .instagram.com/p/CBeZQ47DbUN/.

EPILOGUE. WHY WE CAN'T HAVE NICE THINGS

1 Cronberg, "Branding Authenticity."

2 Richards, "More Luxury Brands."

3 Emphasis added. Lennox, "US Customs Agents Target Counterfeit Goods."

4 If a large portion of fashion knockoffs are produced in Asia, it's because the largest portion of fashion is produced in Asia where garment labor is abundant, cheap, and fast. It's not uncommon to find that a factory is making both branded and copycat goods—and sometimes both the "authentic" and "inauthentic" versions of the same products. See Rodionova, "Alibaba Chief Jack Ma Says Fakes Are Better Quality"; Hoskins, "Luxury Brands"; Wilson, "Fashion Industry Grapples with Designer Knockoffs"; and UK Parliament Environmental Audit Committee, "Fixing Fashion."

5 Lieber, "Instagram Has a Counterfeit Fashion Problem."
6 Lieber, "Instagram Has a Counterfeit Fashion Problem."
7 Graham, "TikTok Teens."
8 Downs, "Is Everyone Buying Fake Bags but Me?"
9 This figure is from "A Women's Replica Community," https://www.reddit.com/r/RepLadies/.
10 This figure is from "Reddit's Source for Replica Discussion," https://www.reddit.com/r/Repsneakers/.
11 Gucci sent Day cease-and-desist letters but never moved forward with a lawsuit against him.
12 Petrarca, "Vetements Outdoes Vetememes."
13 Petrarca, "Diesel Is Opening Its Own Knockoff Pop-Up."
14 Yang, *Faked in China*, 66.
15 hooks, "Eating the Other."

Abbas, Ackbar. "Faking Globalization." In *Other Cities, Other Worlds: Urban Imaginaries in a Globalizing Age*, edited by Andreas Huyssen, 243–66. Durham, NC: Duke University Press, 2008.

Adler, Amy, and Jeanne C. Fromer. "Taking Intellectual Property into Their Own Hands." *California Law Review* 107 (2019): 1455–1530.

Anderson, Jane E. *Law, Knowledge, Culture: The Production of Indigenous Knowledge in Intellectual Property Law*. Cheltenham, UK: Edward Elgar, 2009.

Antik Batik SASU v. I.M. Production SAS. Tribunal de grande instance de Paris, 3rd Chamber 4th Section, 3 December 2015, No 15/03456 | Doctrine.

Aoki, Keith. "Foreign-ness and Asian American Identities: Yellowface, World War II Propaganda, and Bifurcated Racial Stereotypes." *UCLA Asian Pacific American Law Journal* 4, no. 1 (1996): 1–71.

Aoki, Keith. "(Intellectual) Property and Sovereignty: Notes toward a Cultural Geography of Authorship." *Stanford Law Review* 48, no. 5 (1996): 1293–355.

Aoki, Keith. "Neocolonialism, Anticommons Property, and Biopiracy in the (Not-so-Brave) New World Order of Intellectual Property Protection." *Indiana Journal of Global Legal Studies* 6, no. 1 (1998): 11–58.

Aoki, Keith. "The Yellow Pacific: Transnational Identities, Diasporic Racialization, and Myth(s) of the 'Asian Century.'" *UC Davis Law Review* 44 (2011): 897–952.

Arnett, George. "Valentino Is Luxury Fashion's Fastest-Growing Company." *Vogue Business*. May 6, 2019. https://www.voguebusiness.com/companies/fastest-growing-luxury-companies.

Arreola, Veronica. "Latinas: We're So Hot We Broke the Internet." *Ms.* October 13, 2010. http://msmagazine.com/blog/2010/10/13/latinas-were-so-hot-we-broke-google/.

Asia News Network. "Thai Handbags Not Breaking Intellectual Property Laws: IP Chief." March 8, 2016. http://www.asianews.eu/content/thai-handbags-not-breaking-intellectual-property-laws-ip-chief-11036.

Bangkok Post. "'Rainbow Tote' Latest Fashion Statement." March 8, 2016. https://www.bangkokpost.com/life/social-and-lifestyle/890188/rainbow-tote-latest-fashion-statement.

Barry, Colleen. "Dolce & Gabbana Seeks over $600M Damages from 2 US Bloggers." *AP News*. March 7, 2021. https://apnews.com/article/lifestyle-milan-boycotts-asia-26f639d44796a5aa5ae9673bd988b46f.

Barua, Akrur. "Asia's Retail Spending Boom." Deloitte Insights. March 28, 2017. https://www2.deloitte.com/insights/us/en/economy/asia-pacific-economic-outlook/2017/q2-asia-retail-spending-boom.html#endnote-sup-1.

Bell, Derrick. *Faces at the Bottom of the Well: The Permanence of Racism*. New York: Basic Books, 1993.

Benjamin, Ruja. *Race after Technology: Abolitionist Tools for the New Jim Code*. Cambridge, MA: Polity, 2019.

Binkley, Christina. "From the Runway to Your Laptop." *Wall Street Journal*. October 1, 2009. https://www.wsj.com/articles/SB10001424052748704471504574445222739373290.

Blakley, Johanna. "Lessons from Fashion's Free Culture." TED.com. April 2010. https://www.ted.com/talks/johanna_blakley_lessons_from_fashion_s_free_culture.

Boateng, Boatema. *The Copyright Thing Doesn't Work Here: Adinkra and Kente Cloth and Intellectual Property in Ghana*. Minneapolis: University of Minnesota Press, 2011.

Bollier, David, and Laurie Racine. "Ready to Share: Creativity in Fashion and Digital Culture." In *Ready to Share: Fashion and the Ownership of Creativity*. Los Angeles: Norman Lear Center, January 29, 2005.

boyd, danah. "Social Network Sites as Networked Publics: Affordances, Dynamics, and Implications." In *A Networked Self: Identity, Community, and Culture on Social Network Sites*, edited by Zizi Papacharissi, 39–58. New York: Routledge, 2011.

Boyle, Katherine. "Christian Louboutin sues Yves Saint Laurent over red soles on heels." *Washington Post*. April 14, 2011. https://www.washingtonpost.com/lifestyle/style/christian-louboutin-sues-yves-saint-laurent-over-red-soles-on-heels/2011/04/14/AFV2Z4eD_story.html.

Bradsher, Keith. "Chinese Apparel Makers Increasingly Seek the Creative Work." *New York Times*. August 31, 2005: C1.

Branigan, Tania. "China's Taste for High-End Fashion and Luxury Brands Reaches New Heights." *Guardian*. April 26, 2011. https://www.theguardian.com/world/2011/apr/26/china-super-rich-demand-luxury-brands.

Brannigan, Maura. "Condé Nast Bans Terry Richardson from Its Publications." *Fashionista*. October 24, 2017. https://fashionista.com/2017/10/terry-richardson-vogue-conde-nast-banned.

Bromwich, Jonah Engel. "We're All Drinking Diet Prada Now." *New York Times*. March 14, 2019. https://www.nytimes.com/2019/03/14/fashion/diet-prada.html.

Brooks, David. "Stuff and Nonsense." *New York Times*. November 18, 2003: A25.

Bukszpan, Daniel. "Counterfeiting: Many Risks and Many Victims." CNBC. July 13, 2010. http://www.cnbc.com/id/38229835#.

Bush, George W. "A Nation Challenged: Excerpts from the President's Remarks on the War on Terrorism." *New York Times*. October 12, 2001: B4.

Business of Fashion. "What Are the Consequences of Copycats?" March 14, 2016. https://www.businessoffashion.com/community/voices/discussions/what-is-the-real-cost-of-copycats/fashions-copycat-economy.

Business of Fashion and McKinsey and Company. "The State of Fashion: 2018." https://cdn.businessoffashion.com/reports/The_State_of_Fashion_2018_v2.pdf.

Chander, Anupam, and Madhavi Sunder. "The Romance of the Public Domain." *California Law Review* 92, no. 5 (2004): 1331–73.

Chang, Iris. *The Chinese in America: A Narrative History*. New York: Penguin, 2003.

Chen, Adrian. "The Laborers Who Keep Dick Pics and Beheadings Out of Your Facebook Feed." *Wired*. October 23, 2014. https://www.wired.com/2014/10/content-moderation/.

Chow-White, Peter A. "The Informationalization of Race: Communication, Databases, and the Digital Coding of the Genome." *International Journal of Communication* 2 (2008): 1168–94.

Clifford, Stephanie. "Economic Indicator: Even Cheaper Knockoffs." *New York Times*. August 1, 2010: A1.

Cline, Elizabeth. *Overdressed: The Shockingly High Cost of Cheap Fashion*. New York: Penguin, 2012.

Clover, Charles. "Alibaba's Jack Ma Says Fakes Are Better Than Originals." *Financial Times*. June 14, 2016. https://www.ft.com/content/6700d5cc-3209-11e6-ad39-3fee5ffe5b5b.

Colman, Charles E. "The History and Principles of American Copyright Protection for Fashion Design: A Strange Centennial." *Harvard Journal of Sports and Entertainment Law* 6, no. 2 (2015): 225–98.

Colon, Ana. "This Design from Forever 21 Looks Suspiciously Familiar." Refinery29. August 8, 2016. http://www.refinery29.com/2016/08/119392/forever21-sporty-and-rich-knockoff.

Contreras, Milly. "Isabel Marant and Antik Batik Lose Case over Oaxacan Plagiarism Scandal." *LatinPost.com*. December 8, 2015. https://www.latinpost.com/articles/100430/20151208/isabel-marant-and-antik-batik-lose-case-over-oaxacan-plagiarism-scandal.htm.

Cook, Grace. "Why South Korea Is the Home of Counterfeit Culture." *Business of Fashion*. August 24, 2017. https://www.businessoffashion.com/articles/news-analysis/highsnobiety-releases-documentary-on-south-koreas-counterfeit-culture.

Coombe, Rosemary J. *The Cultural Life of Intellectual Properties: Authorship, Appropriation, and the Law*. Durham, NC: Duke University Press, 1998.

Coombe, Rosemary J. "Culture: Anthropology's Old Vice or International Law's New Virtue?" *Proceedings of the Annual Meeting (American Society of International Law)* 93 (1999): 261–70.

Coombe, Rosemary J., and Andrew Herman. "Culture Wars on the Internet: Intellectual Property and Corporate Propriety in Digital Environments." *South Atlantic Quarterly* 100, no. 4 (2001): 919–47.

Coombe, Rosemary J., and Andrew Herman. "Trademarks, Property, and Propriety: The Moral Economy of Consumer Politics and Corporate Accountability on the World Wide Web." *DePaul Law Review* 50, no. 2 (2000): 597–632.

Copping, Nicola. "Style Bloggers Take Centre Stage." *Financial Times*. November 13, 2009. https://www.ft.com/content/89f8c07c-cfe0-11de-a36d-00144feabdc0.

Cornelius, Helen. "American Designer Movement." *Journal of Home Economics* (1934): 500–501.

Coscarelli, Alyssa. "Here's What Happened When We Bought Clothes from Those Sketchy Online Sites." *Refinery 29*. June 27, 2017. https://www.refinery29.com/en-us/2015/11/96886/shopping-asian-e-commerce-style-websites.

Coscarelli, Alyssa. "12 Fashion Knockoffs That Made Our Jaws Drop This Year." *Refinery 29*. December 23, 2016. https://www.refinery29.com/en-us/worst-knockoff-clothing-accessories.

Counterfeit Culture documentary, dir. Geoff D'Eon and Jay Dahl, Telltale Productions, 2013.

Cronberg, Anja Aronowsky. "Branding Authenticity." *Vestoj*. January 15, 2018. http://vestoj.com/branding-anarchy/.

Davey-Attlee, Florence. "Why China Is Sitting on Fashion's Front Row." CNN. February 26, 2013. https://edition.cnn.com/2013/02/26/world/asia/china-london-fashion-week.

Dazed Digital. "I Watched D&G's China Show Fall Apart from the Inside." November 23, 2018. https://www.dazeddigital.com/fashion/article/42334/1/dolce-gabbana-dg-china-cancelled-shanghai-show-model-experience.

Dean, Jodi. *Democracy and Other Neoliberal Fantasies: Communicative Capitalism and Left Politics*. Durham, NC: Duke University Press, 2009.

Dery, Mark. "Culture Jamming: Hacking, Slashing, and Sniping in the Empire of Signs, a Brief Introduction to the 2010 Reprint." October 8, 2010. http://markdery.com/?page_id=154.

Dery, Mark. "The Merry Pranksters and the Art of the Hoax." *New York Times*. December 23, 1990: section 2-1.

Dodd, Philip. "China Chic, Not China Cheap." *Guardian*. December 3, 2005. https://www.theguardian.com/business/2005/dec/04/china.retail.

Dorking, Marie-Claire. "Why Social Media Shaming Is Calling Out Fashion Copycats." *Yahoo News*. March 16, 2016. https://news.yahoo.com/why-social-media-shaming-is-calling-out-fashion-122638189.html.

Dou, Eva. "Jack Ma Says Fakes 'Better Quality and Better Price Than the Real Names.'" *Wall Street Journal*. June 15, 2016. https://blogs.wsj.com/chinarealtime/2016/06/15/jack-ma-says-fakes-better-quality-and-better-price-than-the-real-names/.

Dowd, Maureen. "The Vampire Is Vegan." *New York Times*. April 21, 2019: ST1.

Downs, Claire. "Is Everyone Buying Fake Bags but Me?" *Elle*. January 22, 2020. https://www.elle.com/fashion/a30627106/repladies-reddit-fake-bags/.

Drucker, Peter F. "Japan's Choices." *Foreign Affairs*. Summer 1987. https://www.foreignaffairs.com/articles/asia/1987-06-01/japans-choices.

Duffy, Brooke Erin. *(Not) Getting Paid to Do What You Love: Gender, Social Media, and Aspirational Work*. New Haven, CT: Yale University Press, 2017.

Economist. "Long-Term Chinese Immigrants in Italy." May 17, 2018. https://www.economist.com/special-report/2018/05/17/long-term-chinese-immigrants-in-italy.

Edwards, Jess. "This Designer Bag Looks Like a Plastic Shopping Bag and Instagram Is LOVING It." *Cosmopolitan*. March 9, 2016. https://www.cosmopolitan.com/uk/fashion/style/news/a41815/balenciaga-stripe-shopping-bag-thailand-instagram/.

Ellis, Kristi. "Report Sees China Counterfeiting Worsen." *Women's Wear Daily*. May 1, 2007: 2.

Emarketer.com. "Ecommerce Continues Strong Gains amid Global Economic Uncertainty." June 30, 2019. https://www.emarketer.com/content/ecommerce-continues-strong-gains-amid-global-economic-uncertainty.

Ewick, Patricia, and Susan S. Silbey, eds. *The Common Place of Law: Stories from Everyday Life*. Chicago: University of Chicago Press, 1998.

Faris, Stephan. "Can a Tribe Sue for Copyright? The Maasai Want Royalties for Use of Their Name." Bloomberg.com. October 25, 2013. https://www.bloomberg.com/news/articles/2013-10-24/africas-maasai-tribe-seek-royalties-for-commercial-use-of-their-name.

Farley, Amy. "How the Diet Prada Cofounders Became the Fashion Industry's Most Influential Watchdogs." *Fast Company*. May 22, 2019. https://www.fastcompany.com/90345174/most-creative-people-2019-diet-prada-tony-liu-lindsey-schuyler.

Fashion Law. "Are Your 'Made in China' Luxury Goods Just as Luxurious?" February 14, 2018. http://www.thefashionlaw.com/home/are-your-made-in-china-luxury-goods-just-as-luxurious.

Fashion Law. "Isabel Marant Wins Case over 'Stolen' Tribal Design." December 7, 2015. http://www.thefashionlaw.com/home/isabel-marant-wins-case-over-stolen-tribal-design.

Fashion Originators' Guild of America v. FTC, 312 US 457 (1941).

Fernquest, Jon. "Fashion: Thai Rainbow Bag Scores Big." *Bangkok Post*. March 9, 2016. https://www.bangkokpost.com/learning/advanced/891628/fashion-thai-rainbow-bag-scores-big.

Ferrier, Lindsay. "This Is What Happens When You Order Ridiculously Cheap Clothing from Singapore." *Huffington Post*. December 7, 2017. https://www.huffpost.com/entry/this-is-what-happens-when-you-order-ridiculously-cheap-clothing-from-singapore_b_6249572.

Forster, Katie. "Disappointed Customers Expose Cheap Clothing 'Scams' by Sharing Online Shopping Nightmares." *Independent*. April 9, 2016. https://www.independent.co.uk/news/business/news/disappointed-customers-expose-cheap-clothing-scams-by-sharing-online-shopping-nightmares-a6975201.html.

Foucault, Michel. *Abnormal: Lectures at the Collège de France, 1974–1975*. New York: Picador, 2003.

Frankel, Susannah. "Ready to Wear: Is It Fair to Lambast Such an Innovative Designer in This Way?" *Independent.* June 29, 2009. http://www.independent .co.uk/life-style/fashion/features/ready-to-wear-is-it-fair-to-lambast-such-an -innovative-designer-in-this-way-1722692.html.

Fredriksson, Martin. "Piracy, Globalisation, and the Colonisation of the Commons." *Global Media Journal Australian Edition* 6, no. 1 (2012): 1–10.

Friedman, Vanessa. "Fashion Brands Learn How to Survive a Storm." *New York Times.* June 13, 2019: D1.

Friedman, Vanessa. "The Resurrection of Dolce & Gabbana." *New York Times.* June 12, 2019. https://www.nytimes.com/2019/06/12/fashion/dolce-gabbana -resurrection.html.

Friedman, Vanessa, and Elizabeth Paton. "A Scapegoat for the Fashion Industry?" *New York Times.* October 29, 2017: ST1.

Gana, Ruth. "The Myth of Development, the Progress of Rights: Human Rights to Intellectual Property and Development." *Law and Policy* 18, nos. 3 and 4 (1996): 315–54.

Gerrie, Vanessa. "The Diet Prada Effect: 'Call Out' Culture in the Contemporary Fashion-scape." Paper presented at Fashion, Costume and Visual Cultures Conference, University of Zagreb, Croatia, July 17–18, 2018.

Gillespie, Tarleton. "The Relevance of Algorithms." In *Media Technologies: Essays on Communication, Materiality, and Society*, edited by Tarleton Gillespie, Pablo J. Boczkowski, and Kirsten Frost, 167–94. Cambridge, MA: MIT Press, 2014.

Gino, Francesca, Michael I. Norton, and Dan Ariely. "The Counterfeit Self: The Deceptive Costs of Faking It." *Psychological Science* 21, no. 5 (2010): 712–20.

Glickman, Lawrence B. "'Buy for the Sake of the Slave': Abolitionism and the Origins of American Consumer Activism." *American Quarterly* 56, no. 4 (2004): 889–912.

Glickman, Lawrence B. "'Make Lisle the Style': The Politics of Fashion in the Japanese Silk Boycott, 1937–1940." *Journal of Social History* 38, no. 3 (2005): 573–608.

Gonzalez, Vernadette V., and Robyn Magalit Rodriguez. "Filipinas.com: Wives, Workers, and Whores on the Cyberfrontier." In *AsianAmerica.Net: Ethnicity, Nationalism, and Cyberspace*, edited by Rachel C. Lee and Sau-ling Cynthia Wong, 215–34. New York: Routledge, 2003.

Gosline, Renee Richardson. "The Real Value of Fakes: Dynamic Symbolic Boundaries in Socially Embedded Consumption." Dissertation. Harvard Business School, 2009.

Graafland, Amber. "How Balenciaga's £975 Thai Market Stall–Inspired Bag Became This Season's Surprise Best Seller." *Mirror*. April 19, 2017. https://www

.mirror.co.uk/3am/style/celebrity-fashion/how-balenciagas-975-thai-market
-10254783.

Graham, Megan. "TikTok Teens Are Obsessed with Fake Luxury Products." CNBC.
March 1, 2020. https://www.cnbc.com/2020/02/29/tiktok-teens-are-obsessed
-with-fake-luxury-products.html.

Green, Joshua. "Bannon's Back and Targeting China." *Bloomberg*. September 28,
2017. https://www.bloomberg.com/news/articles/2017-09-28/bannon-s-back
-and-targeting-china.

Greene, K. J. "'Copynorms,' Black Cultural Production, and the Debate over African American Reparations." *Cardoza Arts and Entertainment Law Journal* 25,
no. 3 (2008): 1179-227.

Hall, Casey. "Cracks Appear in China's Fashion Magazine Landscape." *Business
of Fashion*. November 14, 2018. https://www.businessoffashion.com/articles
/professional/cracks-appear-in-chinas-fashion-magazine-landscape.

Hall, Casey. "A Turning Point for China's Stance on Counterfeit Luxury Goods."
Business of Fashion. December 11, 2018. https://www.businessoffashion.com
/articles/global-currents/a-turning-point-for-chinas-stance-on-counterfeit
-luxury-goods.

Harney, Alexandra. "China's Copycat Culture." *New York Times*. October 31, 2011.
https://latitude.blogs.nytimes.com/2011/10/31/chinas-copycat-culture/.

Harold, Christine. "Pranking Rhetoric: 'Culture Jamming' as Media Activism."
Critical Studies in Media Communication 21, no. 3 (2004): 189-211.

Harris, Cheryl. "Whiteness as Property." *Harvard Law Review* 106, no. 8
(June 1993): 1707-91.

Hawes, Elizabeth. *Fashion Is Spinach*. New York: Random House, 1938.

Hemphill, C. Scott, and Jeannie Suk. "The Fashion Originators' Guild of America:
Self-Help at the Edge of IP and Antitrust." In *Intellectual Property at the Edge:
The Contested Contours of IP*, edited by Rochelle Cooper Dreyfuss and Jane C.
Ginsburg, 159-79. Cambridge: Cambridge University Press, 2014.

Herbert, Wray. "We're Only Human: Faking It." *Scientific American* 21, no. 4 (September 2010): 66-67.

Hernitaningtyas, Keshie. "This Is Why Balenciaga's Latest Tote Bags Are Trending." *Jakarta Post*. March 21, 2016. https://www.thejakartapost.com/life/2016
/03/15/this-is-why-balenciagas-latest-tote-bags-are-trending.html.

Higgins, Kathy. "Use Your Buying Power for Justice: The League of Women Shoppers and Innocuous Feminist Radicalism 1935-1948." *Chicago Journal of History*
(Spring 2016): 44-53.

Hines, Alice. "Forever 21 under Investigation for Using 'Sweatshop-Like' Factories
in Los Angeles." *Huffington Post*. October 26, 2012. https://www.huffpost.com
/entry/forever-21-sweatshop-investigation_n_2025390.

hooks, bell. "Eating the Other: Desire and Resistance." In *Black Looks: Race and
Representation*, 21-40. Boston: South End Press, 1992.

Hoskins, Tansy. "Luxury Brands: Higher Standards or Just a Higher Mark-Up?" *Guardian*. December 10, 2014. https://www.theguardian.com/sustainable -business/2014/dec/10/luxury-brands-behind-gloss-same-dirt-ethics -production.

Irani, Lilly. "Justice for 'Data Janitors.'" Public Books (blog). January 15, 2015. https://www.publicbooks.org/justice-for-data-janitors/#fn-1757-7.

Isaac-Goizé, Tina. "They Only Skimped on the Fabric." *New York Times*. December 4, 2016: ST12.

Jablow, Arthur. Interview on May 14, 1982. Memoirs of Maurice Rentner from Varying Perspectives, Special Collections and College Archives, Oral History Project of the Fashion Industries, Fashion Institute of Technology, New York.

James, Lydia. "The Diet Prada Effect." Lydia (blog). January 2018. https://lydia -1999.blogspot.com/2018/01/the-diet-prada-effect_24.html.

Jarrett, Kylie. *Feminism, Labour, and Digital Media: The Digital Housewife*. New York: Routledge, 2016.

Johns, Adrian. *Piracy: The Intellectual Property Wars from Gutenberg to Gates*. Chicago: University of Chicago Press, 2010.

Johnson v. M'Intosh, 21 US 543, 573 (1823).

Jung-a, Song. "Luxury Brands Battle to Stay in Fashion in South Korea." CNBC. June 23, 2014. https://www.cnbc.com/2014/06/23/luxury-brands-battle-to-stay -in-fashion-in-south-korea.html.

Kacynski, Andrew. "Carly Fiorina: The Chinese 'Can't Innovate, Not Terribly Imaginative, Not Entrepreneurial.'" *Buzzfeed*. May 26, 2015. https://www .buzzfeed.com/andrewkaczynski/carly-fiorina-the-chinese-cant-innovate-not -terribly-imagina?utm_term=.qxwwrNKYK#.qbZOzLAqA.

Kaplan, Isaac. "How Artists Are Fighting Back against the Fashion Industry's Plagiarism Problem." Artsy.net. September 19, 2016. https://www.artsy.net/article /artsy-editorial-how-artists-are-fighting-back-against-the-fashion-industry-s -plagiarism-problem.

Karabell, Shellie. "Too Much Demand, Too Little Space: Chinese Vogue." *Forbes*. November 30, 2011. https://www.forbes.com/sites/insead/2011/11/30/too-much -demand-too-little-space-chinese-vogue/#1737dc174ce3.

Katz, Evan Ross. "Diet Prada Elevates Dolce & Gabbana Feud by Setting the Label on Fire, Literally." Mic.com. January 5, 2018. https://www.mic.com/articles /187238/diet-prada-elevates-dolce-and-gabbana-feud-by-setting-the-label-on -fire-literally.

Khagi, Irina Oberman. "Who's Afraid of Forever 21? Combating Copycatting through Extralegal Enforcement of Moral Rights in Fashion Designs." *Fordham Intellectual Property, Media and Entertainment Law Journal* 27, no. 1 (2016): 65–102.

Kim, Elaine H. "Asian Americans and American Popular Culture." In *Dictionary of Asian American History*, edited by Hyung-Chan Kim, 99–116. Westport, CT: Greenwood Press, 1986.

Kitroeff, Natalie. "Factories That Made Clothes for Forever 21, Ross Paid Workers $4 an Hour, Labor Department Says." *Los Angeles Times*. November 16, 2016. https://www.latimes.com/business/la-fi-wage-theft-forever-ross-20161116-story.html.

Kitroeff, Natalie, and Victoria Kim. "Behind a $13 Shirt, a $6-an-Hour Worker." *Los Angeles Times*. August 31, 2017. https://www.latimes.com/projects/la-fi-forever-21-factory-workers/.

Klein, Ezra. "Copycats vs. Copyrights." *Newsweek*. August 20, 2010. https://www.newsweek.com/copycats-vs-copyrights-71361.

Klein, Naomi. *No Logo*. New York: Picador, 1999.

Lacy, Lisa. "Why 2018 Was the 'Year of Ecommerce' in Southeast Asia." *Adweek*. December 3, 2018. https://www.adweek.com/digital/why-2018-was-the-year-of-ecommerce-in-southeast-asia/.

Lanigan, Roisin. "The Duo behind Diet Prada Speak Publicly for the First Time." *I-D Vice*. May 8, 2018. https://i-d.vice.com/en_us/article/a3awzp/the-duo-behind-diet-prada-speak-publicly-for-the-first-time.

Larocca, Amy. "Fashion Police." *New York*. April 29, 2002. http://nymag.com/nymetro/shopping/fashion/features/5938/.

Larsson, Naomi. "Inspiration or Plagiarism? Mexicans Seek Reparations for French Designer's Look-Alike Blouse." *Guardian*. June 17, 2015. https://www.theguardian.com/global-development-professionals-network/2015/jun/17/mexican-mixe-blouse-isabel-marant.

Lasn, Kalle. *Culture Jam: The Uncooling of America*. New York: Eagle Brook, 1999.

Lazzarato, Maurizio. "Immaterial Labor." In *Radical Thought in Italy: A Potential Politics*, edited by Paolo Virno and Michael Hardy, 133–50. Minneapolis: University of Minnesota Press, 2006.

Lazzaro, Sage. "All Signs Point to Scam for Those Trendy Clothes Sites Flooding Facebook with Ads." *Observer*. September 17, 2015. https://observer.com/2015/09/all-signs-point-to-scam-for-those-trendy-clothes-sites-flooding-facebook-with-ads/.

Lennox, Jeff. "US Customs Agents Target Counterfeit Goods with Mandatory Screening." 7 News Miami. February 18, 2020. https://wsvn.com/news/local/us-customs-agents-target-counterfeit-goods-with-mandatory-screening/.

Lessig, Lawrence. *Free Culture: How Big Media Uses Technology and the Law to Lock Down Culture and Control Creativity*. New York: Penguin, 2004.

Liao, Sara. *Fashioning China: Precarious Creativity and Women Designers in Shanzhai Culture*. London: Pluto, 2020.

Lieber, Chavie. "Fashion Brands Steal Design Ideas All the Time." *Vox*. April 27, 2018. https://www.vox.com/2018/4/27/17281022/fashion-brands-knockoffs-copyright-stolen-designs-old-navy-zara-h-and-m.

Lieber, Chavie. "Instagram Has a Counterfeit Fashion Problem." *Vox*. May 2, 2019. https://www.vox.com/the-goods/2019/5/2/18527181/instagram-counterfeit-industry-chanel-gucci-louis-vuitton.

Lieber, Chavie. "Why the $600 Billion Counterfeit Industry Is Still Horrible for Fashion." *Racked*. December 1, 2014. https://www.racked.com/2014/12/1/7566859/counterfeit-fashion-goods-products-museum-exhibit.

Lipsitz, George. *The Possessive Investment in Whiteness: How White People Profit from Identity Politics*. Philadelphia: Temple University Press, 1998.

Lipsky-Karasz, Elisa. "Karl Lagerfeld Was Never Satisfied." *Wall Street Journal Magazine*. February 13, 2017. https://www.wsj.com/articles/karl-lagerfeld-is-never-satisfied-1487001657.

London, Jack. *Revolution and Other Essays*. London: Macmillan, 1910.

Los Angeles Times. "Japanese in U.S. Outdo Horatio Alger." October 17, 1977: 1.

Luvaas, Brent. "Designer Vandalism: Indonesian Indie Fashion and the Cultural Practice of Cut 'n' Paste." *Visual Anthropology Review* 26, no. 1 (2010): 1–16.

Luvaas, Brent. "Material Interventions: Indonesian DIY Fashion and the Regime of the Global Brand." *Cultural Anthropology* 28, no. 1 (2013): 127–43.

Lye, Colleen. *America's Asia: Racial Form and American Literature, 1893–1945*. Princeton, NJ: Princeton University Press, 2004.

Magni, Max, and Yuval Atsmon. "China's Luxury Consumers Grow Up." *Harvard Business Review*. April 12, 2011. https://hbr.org/2011/04/chinas-luxury-consumers-grow-u.

Malay Mail. "Why Thais Are Having a Good Chuckle over Balenciaga's New 'It' Bag." March 10, 2016. https://www.malaymail.com/news/life/2016/03/10/why-thais-are-having-a-good-chuckle-over-balenciagas-new-bag/1077151.

Marcketti, Sara Beth. "Design Piracy in the United States Women's Ready-to-Wear Apparel Industry: 1910–1941." Unpublished dissertation. Iowa State University, 2005.

Marcketti, Sara B., and Jean L. Parsons. "Design Piracy and Self-Regulation: The Fashion Originators' Guild of America, 1932–1941." *Clothing and Textiles Research Journal* 24, no. 3 (2006): 214–28.

Marshall, Jack. "Companies Increasingly Trademark Hashtags." *Wall Street Journal*. March 30, 2016. https://www.wsj.com/articles/companies-increasingly-trademark-hashtags-1459333936.

Marwick, Alice, and danah boyd. "To See and Be Seen: Celebrity Practice on Twitter." *Convergence: The International Journal of Research into New Media Technologies* 17, no. 2 (2011): 139–58.

Masnick, Mike. "Hey NY Times: Can You Back Up the Claim of $200 Billion Lost to Counterfeiting?" *TechDirt*. August 2, 2010. https://www.techdirt.com/articles/20100801/17431810439.shtml.

Master, Farah. "Bottom Line: Brands Chase China's High-End Lingerie Market." *Reuters*. July 23, 2016. https://www.reuters.com/article/us-china-lingerie/bottom-line-brands-chase-chinas-high-end-lingerie-market-idUSKCN104024.

Mau, Dhani. "Valentino Is the Latest Brand to Drop Terry Richardson." *Fashionista*. October 24, 2017. https://fashionista.com/2017/10/terry-richardson-work-dropped-brands.

McDowell, Maghan. "Protecting Fashion Hashtags with Trademarks." *Women's Wear Daily*. April 6, 2016. https://wwd.com/business-news/media/fashion-hashtag-trademark-10404235/.

Meiklejohn, Helen Everett. "Dresses—the Impact of Fashion on a Business." In *Price and Price Policies*, edited by Walton Hamilton, 338–39. New York: McGraw Hill, 1938.

Menkes, Suzy. "The Asian Wave." *New York Times*. February 8, 2013. https://www.nytimes.com/2013/02/09/fashion/the-asian-wave-in-fashion.html.

Metcalfe, Jessica. "Misappropriation and the Case of the Yellow Crotch." *Beyond Buckskin* (blog). January 22, 2013. http://www.beyondbuckskin.com/2013/01/misappropriation-and-case-of-yellow.html.

Midler, Paul. *Poorly Made in China: An Insider's Account of the China Production Game*. Hoboken, NJ: Wiley and Sons, 2009.

Mirghani, Suzannah. "The War on Piracy: Analyzing the Discursive Battles of Corporate and Government-Sponsored Anti-piracy Media Campaigns." *Critical Studies in Media Communication* 28, no. 2 (2011): 113–34.

Morley, David, and Kevin Robins. *Spaces of Identity*. London: Routledge, 1995.

Murphy, Candace. "Mass Couture." *East Bay Times*. November 13, 2005. https://www.eastbaytimes.com/2005/11/13/mass-couture/.

Nakamura, Lisa. "The Unwanted Labour of Social Media: Women of Color Call Out Culture as Venture Community Management." *New Formations: A Journal of Culture, Theory, Politics* 86 (2015): 106–12.

Nakassis, Constantine V. "Brands and Their Surfeits." *Cultural Anthropology* 28, no. 1 (2013): 111–26.

Nakassis, Constantine V. "The Quality of a Copy." In *Fashion India: Spectacular Capitalism*, edited by Tereza Kuldova, 142–65. Trondheim: Fagbokforlaget, 2013.

NBC News. "Dolce & Gabbana Fiasco Shows Importance, Risks of China Market." November 27, 2018. https://www.nbcnews.com/news/asian-america/dolce-gabbana-fiasco-shows-importance-risks-china-market-n940706.

Newman, Louise Michele. *White Women's Rights: The Racial Origins of Feminism in the United States*. New York: Oxford University Press, 1999.

Newsweek. "Success Story: Outwhiting the Whites." July 21, 1971.

New York Times. "Hits Garment Practices." October 29, 1936.

Noble, Safiya Umoja. *Algorithms of Oppression: How Search Engines Reinforce Racism*. New York: New York University Press, 2018.

Noble, Safiya Umoja. "Missed Connections: What Search Engines Say about Women." *Bitch Magazine* 54 (Spring 2012): 36–41.

Nystrom, Paul H. *Economics of Fashion*. New York: Ronald Press, 1928.

Odell, Amy. "From the Disco to JCPenney: The Enduring Tragedy of Halston." *The Cut*. December 19, 2011. https://www.thecut.com/2011/12/halston-from-the-disco-to-jcpenney.html.

Oguamanam, Chidi. *International Law and Indigenous Knowledge: Intellectual Property Rights, Plant Biodiversity, and Traditional Medicine*. Toronto: University of Toronto Press, 2006.

Omi, Michael, and Howard Winant. *Racial Formation in the United States: From the 1960s to the 1990s*. New York: Routledge, 1984.

Pang, Laikwan. *Creativity and Its Discontents: China's Creative Industries and Intellectual Property Rights Offenses*. Durham, NC: Duke University Press, 2012.

Pang, Laikwan. *Cultural Control and Globalization in Asia: Copyright, Piracy, and Cinema*. London: Routledge, 2006.

Pasquarelli, Adrianne. "40 Under 40: Shirley Cook, 32." *Crains New York Business*. October 12, 2012. http://www.crainsnewyork.com/40under40/2012/Cook.

Patry, William. *Moral Panics and the Copyright Wars*. New York: Oxford University Press, 2009.

Paul, Kari. "Is Social Media the New Court of Law for Fashion Copycats?" *Market Watch*. June 10, 2017. https://www.marketwatch.com/story/is-social-media-the-new-court-of-law-for-fashion-copycats-2017-06-09.

Perzanowski, Aaron, and Jason Schultz. *The End of Ownership: Personal Property in the Digital Economy*. Cambridge, MA: MIT Press, 2016.

Petersen, William. "Success Story, Japanese American Style." *New York Times Magazine*. January 9, 1966: 20–21.

Petrarca, Emilia. "Diesel Is Opening Its Own Knockoff Pop-Up on Canal Street." *The Cut*. February 8, 2018. https://www.thecut.com/2018/02/diesel-knockoff-collection-canal-street.html.

Petrarca, Emilia. "Vetements Outdoes Vetememes, Produces 'Official Fake' Collection for South Korea." *W Magazine*. October 18, 2016. https://www.wmagazine.com/story/vetements-outdoes-vetememes-produces-official-fake-collection-for-south-korea/.

Pham, Minh-Ha T. *Asians Wear Clothes on the Internet: Race, Gender, and the Work of Personal Style Blogging*. Durham, NC: Duke University Press, 2015.

Pham, Minh-Ha T. "*China Through the Looking Glass*: Race, Property, and the Possessive Investment in White Feelings." In *Fashion and Beauty in the Time of Asia*, edited by Heijin Lee, Christina H. Moon, and Thuy Linh N. Tu, 41–68. New York: New York University Press, 2019.

Pham, Minh-Ha T. "Fashion's Cultural Appropriation Debate." *The Atlantic*. May 15, 2014. https://www.theatlantic.com/entertainment/archive/2014/05/cultural-appropriation-in-fashion-stop-talking-about-it/370826/.

Pham, Minh-Ha T. "The High Cost of High Fashion." *Jacobin*. June 13, 2017. https://www.jacobinmag.com/2017/06/fast-fashion-labor-prada-gucci-abuse-designer.

Pham, Minh-Ha T. "The Right to Fashion in the Age of Terrorism." *Signs* 36, no. 2 (2011): 385–410.

Philip, Kavita. "What Is a Technological Author? The Pirate Function and Intellectual Property." *Postcolonial Studies* 8, no. 2 (2005): 199–218.

Pike, Helena. "The Copycat Economy." *Business of Fashion*. March 14, 2016. https://www.businessoffashion.com/community/voices/discussions/what-is-the -real-cost-of-copycats/fashions-copycat-economy.

Pink News. "Target Agrees to Fund Gay Groups Following Lady Gaga Deal." February 21, 2011. https://www.pinknews.co.uk/2011/02/21/target-agrees-to-stop -funding-anti-gay-groups-following-lady-gaga-deal/.

Porter, Nia. "You Can Now Buy Balenciaga's 'Laundry Bags' for over $2,000." *Racked*. August 2, 2016. https://www.racked.com/2016/8/2/12351074 /balenciaga-bazar-bags.

Pouillard, Veronique. "Design Piracy in the Fashion Industries of Paris and New York in the Interwar Years." *Business History Review* 85, no. 2 (2011): 319–44.

Qiu, Jack Linchuan. *Working-Class Network Society: Communication Technology and the Information Have-Less in Urban China*. Cambridge, MA: MIT Press, 2009.

Radin, Sara. "How a Copyright Loophole Gave Birth to Fashion's 'Name and Shame' Social Media Pastime." *Observer*. April 30, 2019. https://observer.com /2019/04/copyright-loophole-fashion-social-media-police-diet-prada-copycat/.

Rantisi, Norma M. "The Ascendance of New York Fashion." *International Journal of Urban and Regional Research* 28, no. 1 (2004): 86–106.

Rapp, Jessica. "Two Chinese Copycat Fashion Brands Lose Trademark Battles but War Is Far from Over." *South China Morning Post*. November 26, 2018. https:// www.scmp.com/lifestyle/fashion-beauty/article/2175012/comeuppance-cartier -copycat-cairter-and-dunhill.

Raustiala, Kal, and Christopher Sprigman. *The Knockoff Economy: How Imitation Sparks Innovation*. New York: Oxford University Press, 2012.

Raustiala, Kal, and Christopher Sprigman. "The Piracy Paradox: Innovation and Intellectual Property in Fashion Design." *Virginia Law Review* 92, no. 8 (2006): 1687–777.

Raustiala, Kal, and Christopher Sprigman. "The Piracy Paradox Revisited." *Stanford Law Review* 61, no. 5 (2009): 1201–25.

Reed, Trevor. "Who Owns Our Ancestors' Voices?" *Columbia Journal of Law and the Arts* 40, no. 2 (2017): 275–310.

Reuters. "United States Waking Up to Chinese Abuses, US Senator Elizabeth Warren Says in Beijing." April 1, 2018. https://www.scmp.com/news/china /diplomacy-defence/article/2139809/united-states-waking-chinese-abuses-us -senator.

Richards, Katie. "More Luxury Brands Are Joining TikTok to Combat Dupes." *Glossy*. March 13, 2020. https://www.glossy.co/fashion/more-luxury-brands-are -joining-tiktok-to-combat-dupes.

Ritschel, Chelsea. "Stefano Gabbana: Homosexual Dolce & Gabbana Co-founder Denounces Use of 'Gay' as a Label." *Independent*. December 18, 2017. https:// www.independent.co.uk/life-style/stefano-gabbana-gay-fashion-designer-dolce -d-and-g-homosexual-label-lgbt-a8116791.html.

Robinson, Selma. "America Dresses Herself." *Woman's Home Companion* (1941): 15.

Rodionova, Ziata. "Alibaba Chief Jack Ma Says Fakes Are Better Quality Than Authentic Luxury Goods." *Independent*. June 15, 2016. https://www.independent.co.uk/news/business/news/alibaba-chief-jack-ma-says-fakes-are-better-quality-than-authentic-luxury-goods-a7083236.html.

Salmon, Felix. "All Counterfeiting Statistics Are Bullshit." *FelixSalmon.com* (personal website). June 9, 2005. http://www.felixsalmon.com/2005/06/all-counterfeiting-statistics-are-bullshit/.

Salmon, Felix. "CNBC Embarrasses Itself on Counterfeiting." *Reuters* (blog). July 19, 2010. http://blogs.reuters.com/felix-salmon/2010/07/19/cnbc-embarrasses-itself-on-counterfeiting/.

Salmon, Felix. "Counterfeiting: Much Less Prevalent Than You Think." *FelixSalmon.com* (personal website). October 26, 2007. http://www.felixsalmon.com/2007/10/counterfeiting-much-less-prevalent-than-you-think/.

Sanchez, Julian. "750,000 Lost Jobs? The Dodgy Digits behind the War on Piracy." *Ars Technica*. October 7, 2008. http://arstechnica.com/tech-policy/2008/10/dodgy-digits-behind-the-war-on-piracy/.

Schmidt, Rocky. "Designer Law: Fashioning a Remedy for Design Piracy." *UCLA Law Review* 30 (1983): 861–80.

Schultz, Mark F. "Copynorms: Copyright and Social Norms." In *Intellectual Property and Information Wealth*, vol. 1, edited by Peter K. Yu, 201–36. Westport, CT: Praeger, 2006.

Shenkar, Oded. *The Chinese Century: The Rising Chinese Economy and Its Impact on the Global Economy, the Balance of Power, and Your Job*. Upper Saddle River, NJ: Pearson Education, 2005.

Sherman, Lauren. "Are Fakes Back in Fashion?" *Fashionista*. July 14, 2014. http://fashionista.com/2014/07/fakes-in-fashion.

Sherman, Lauren. "Diet Prada Unmasked." *Business of Fashion*. May 8, 2018. https://www.businessoffashion.com/articles/professional/diet-prada-instagram-unmasked-tony-liu-lindsey-schuyler.

Sherwin, Robert T. "#HaveWeReallyThoughtThisThrough? Why Granting Trademark Protection to Hashtags Is Unnecessary, Duplicative, and Downright Dangerous." *Harvard Journal of Law and Technology* 29, no. 2 (2016): 455–93.

Shiva, Vandana. *Biopiracy: The Plunder of Nature and Knowledge*. Boston: South End Press, 1997.

Silver, Dena. "Proenza Schouler Gets a Major Push from a Minority Investment." *Observer*. June 23, 2015. http://observer.com/2015/06/proenza-schouler-gets-a-major-push-from-a-minority-investment/.

Simpson, Audra. "Consent's Revenge." *Cultural Anthropology* 31, no. 3 (2016): 326–33.

Singapore Business Review. "Asia E-commerce Market Projected to Grow to US $1.6T in 2021." December 4, 2017. https://sbr.com.sg/retail/asia/asia-e-commerce-market-projected-grow-us16t-in-2021.

Sowray, Bibby. "Balenciaga's Striped Bags Are Already #Winning Instagram." *Elle*. August 3, 2016. https://www.elle.com/uk/fashion/articles/a29728/balenciaga -aw16-striped-laundry-bags-instagram-thailand-sampeng-market/.

Soyer, Daniel. "The Rise and Fall of the Garment Industry in New York City." In *A Coat of Many Colors: Immigration, Globalization, and Reform in the New York City Garment Industry*, edited by Daniel Soyer, 3–26. New York: Fordham University Press, 2004.

Spence, Jonathan D. *The Chan's Great Continent: China in Western Minds*. New York: W. W. Norton, 1998.

Spindler, Amy M. "A Ruling by French Court Finds Copyright in a Design." *New York Times*. May 19, 1994: D4.

Stephenson, Lauren Benet, and Rachel Strugatz, "Social Media: The New Front Row of Fashion." *Women's Wear Daily*. February 15, 2010. https://wwd.com /business-news/media/social-media-the-new-front-row-of-fashion-2472526/.

Sun, Brian S. "The Wild, Wild East: Strategies to Combat Counterfeiting in China." *Lexology*. January 3, 2013. http://www.lexology.com/library/detail.aspx ?g=d66f072f-089b-4c01-9319-71f482db9c97.

Sundstrom, William A. "Last Hired, First Fired? Unemployment and Urban Black Workers during the Great Depression." *Journal of Economic History* 52, no. 2 (1992): 415–29.

Szmydke, Paulina. "Isabel Marant Cleared of Plagiarism Allegations." *Women's Wear Daily*. December 7, 2015. http://wwd.com/business-news/legal/isabel -marant-plagiarism-antik-batik-mexico-tlahuitoltepec-paris-10291754/.

Target. "Target Corporation Annual Report: 2018." https://corporate.target.com/ _media/TargetCorp/annualreports/2018/pdfs/2018-Target-Annual-Report.pdf.

Tatlow, Didi Kirsten. "Why Do the Chinese Copy So Much." *New York Times*. June 25, 2012. https://rendezvous.blogs.nytimes.com/2012/07/25/why-do-the -chinese-copy-so-much/.

Taylor, Kate. "Target Quietly Removes a T-shirt from Its Website after Being Accused of 'Stealing the Art of a Gay Mexican Artist.'" *Business Insider*. May 16, 2018. https://www.businessinsider.com/target-accused-of-stealing-design-stops -selling-shirt-2018-5.

Terranova, Tiziana. "Free Labor: Producing Culture for the Digital Economy." *Social Text* 18, no. 2 (2000): 33–58.

Thomas, Amanda. "Balenciaga Casts No Models of Color and Appropriates Cheap Thai Bag." *Runway Riot*. March 10, 2016. http://runwayriot.com/2016 /03/10/balenciaga-casts-no-models-of-color-and-appropriates-cheap-thai -bag/.

Thomas, Dana. *Deluxe: How Luxury Lost Its Luster*. New York: Penguin, 2007.

Thomas, Kedron. *Regulating Style: Intellectual Property Law and the Business of Fashion in Guatemala*. Berkeley: University of California Press, 2016.

Thomas, Lauren. "Store Closures Rocked Retail in 2017. Now 2018 Is Set to Bring Another Round of Them." CNBC. December 26, 2017. https://www.cnbc.com

/2017/12/26/store-closures-rocked-retail-in-2017-and-more-should-come-next
-year.html.

Tirrell, Meg. "Fake Louis Vuitton Bags Look Fake without a Tony Aura."
Bloomberg. December 2, 2009. http://www.bloomberg.com/apps/news?pid
=newsarchive&sid=a2goSFXqnqiw.

Trebay, Guy. "At Marc Jacobs, the Show before the Show." *New York Times*. February 17, 2011: E1.

Trebay, Guy. "An Uneasy Cultural Exchange." *New York Times*. March 15,
2012: E1.

Tsosie, Rebecca. "Who Controls Native Cultural Heritage? 'Art,' 'Artifacts,' and the
Right to Cultural Survival." In *Cultural Heritage Issues: The Legacy of Conquest,
Colonization, and Commerce*, edited by James A. R. Nafziger and Ann M.
Nicgorski, 3–36. Leiden, Netherlands: Martinus Nijhoff, 2009.

UK Parliament Environmental Audit Committee. "Fixing Fashion: Clothing
Consumption and Sustainability." February 19, 2019. https://publications
.parliament.uk/pa/cm201719/cmselect/cmenvaud/1952/1952.pdf.

US Copyright Office. "Statement of the United States Copyright Office before the
Subcommittee on Courts, the Internet, and Intellectual Property, Committee
on the Judiciary." July 27, 2006. http://www.copyright.gov/docs/regstat072706
.html.

US Government Accountability Office. "Intellectual Property, Observations on
Efforts to Quantify the Economic Effects of Counterfeit and Pirated Goods."
April 2010. https://www.gao.gov/assets/gao-10-423.pdf.

US Government Accountability Office. "Intellectual Property, Report to the
Ranking Member, Subcommittee on Oversight of Government Management,
the Federal Workforce, and the District of Columbia, Committee on Homeland
Security and Governmental Affairs, US Senate." April 2007. https://www.gao
.gov/assets/gao-07-735.pdf.

US Government Publishing Office. "Innovative Design Protection and Piracy
Prevention Act: Hearing before the Subcommittee on Intellectual Property,
Competition, and the Internet." July 15, 2011. https://www.govinfo.gov/content
/pkg/CHRG-112hhrg67397/html/CHRG-112hhrg67397.htm.

US House of Representatives, Committee on International Relations. "Intellectual
Property Crimes: Are Proceeds from Counterfeited Goods Funding Terrorism?"
Hearing. July 16, 2003. https://www.hsdl.org/?view&did=443961.

US News and World Report. "Success Story of One Minority Group in US." December 26, 1966.

Vann, Elizabeth F. "The Limits of Authenticity in Vietnamese Consumer Markets."
American Anthropologist 108, no. 2 (2006): 286–96.

Varagur, Krithika. "Mexico Prevents Indigenous Designs from Being Culturally Appropriated—Again." *Huffington Post*. March 17, 2016. https://www
.huffingtonpost.com/entry/mexico-prevents-Indigenous-designs-from-being
-culturally-appropriated-again_us_56e87879e4b0b25c9183afc4.

Vats, Anjali. *The Color of Creatorship: Intellectual Property, Race, and the Making of Americans*. Stanford, CA: Stanford University Press, 2020.

Vats, Anjali. "(Dis)Owning Bikram: Decolonizing Vernacular and Dewesternizing Restructuring in the Yoga Wars." *Communication and Critical/Cultural Studies* 13, no. 4 (2016): 1–21.

Vats, Anjali, and Deidre A. Keller. "Critical Race IP." *Cardozo Arts and Entertainment Law Journal* 36, no. 3 (2018): 735–95.

Verklan, Elizabeth. "Doing What You Love in the Age of Mass Debt." *Lateral* 7, no. 1 (2018). https://doi.org/10.25158/L7.1.9.

Vogue. "Piracy on the High Fashions." July 1933: 28, 69.

von Furstenberg, Diane. "Fashion Deserves Copyright Protection." *Los Angeles Times*. August 24, 2007. https://www.latimes.com/opinion/la-oew-furstenberg24aug24-story.html.

Wadler, Joyce. "Remaking the Scene." *New York Times*. December 31, 2008: D1.

Williams, Raymond. *Culture and Materialism: Selected Essays*. London: Verso, 1980.

Williams, Robert. "Dolce & Gabbana Is Still Paying for Insulting Chinese Women." *Bloomberg Businessweek*. March 7, 2019. https://www.bloomberg.com/news/articles/2019–03–07/dolce-gabbana-is-still-paying-for-insulting-chinese-women.

Wilson, Eric. "Before Models Can Turn Around, Knockoffs Fly." *New York Times*. September 4, 2007: A1.

Wilson, Eric. "Fashion Industry Grapples with Designer Knockoffs." *New York Times*. September 4, 2007. https://www.nytimes.com/2007/09/04/business/worldbusiness/04iht-fashion.1.7373169.html.

Wohlsen, Marcus. "Alibaba Now Worth More Than Facebook, Amazon, and IBM." *Wired*. September 22, 2014. http://www.wired.co.uk/article/alibaba-is-already-bigger.

Wolcott, Clarissa. "Adolf Hitler: Grand Couturier." *Living Age* (June 1941): 327.

Women's Wear Daily. "Formal Turbans and Square Crowns Guild Millinery Selections." September 8, 1932: 45.

Women's Wear Daily. "Guild Not to Copy Models of Retailers." April 11, 1935: 26.

Women's Wear Daily. "$1.37 to $6.75 Dress Concerns Condemn Code Style Program." August 30, 1934: 1.

Women's Wear Daily. "Protecting Originality." January 22, 1932: section 1: 9.

Women's Wear Daily. "6 Pickets Arrested in New Orleans." September 20, 1960: 52.

Yang, Fan. *Faked in China: Nation Branding, Counterfeit Culture, and Globalization*. Bloomington: Indiana University Press, 2015.

Yi, David. "How Social Media Shaming Controls Fashion Copycats." *Mashable*. March 15, 2016. https://mashable.com/2016/03/15/fashion-copying-social-media/.

Yin, Cao. "Alibaba Vows to Carry On Fake Goods Crackdown." *China Daily*. May 17, 2016. https://www.chinadaily.com.cn/china/2016–05/17/content_25330721.htm.

Yucatan Times. "Indigenous Oaxacans Challenge French Label over Clothing Design Patent." November 23, 2015. http://www.theyucatantimes.com/2015/11 /Indigenous-oaxacans-challenge-french-label-over-clothing-designs/.

Zakkour, Michael. "Copycat China Still a Problem for Brands and China's Future." *Forbes.* April 30, 3014. https://www.forbes.com/sites/michaelzakkour/2014/04 /30/copycat-china-still-a-problem-for-brands-chinas-future-just-ask-apple -hyatt-starbucks/?sh=164335bb2156.

Zane, Zachary. "This Dolce & Gabbana T-shirt Reeks of Internalized Homophobia." *Pride.com.* December 27, 2017. https://www.pride.com/style/2017/12/27 /dolce-gabbana-t-shirt-reeks-internalized-homophobia.

Zargani, Luisa, and Tiffany Ap. "Dolce & Gabbana: Assessing the Fallout." *Women's Wear Daily.* November 25, 2018. https://wwd.com/fashion-news /fashion-features/dolce-gabbana-surviving-china-controversy-1202912436/.